I'm a Little Brain Dead

by
Kimberly Davis Basso

Printed in the United States of America
First printing, 2018

ISBN-13: 978-0-692-09586-7

www.KimberlyDavisBasso.com

Back cover photo credit:
Donna Alberico
www.DonnaAlberico.com

To the clots.
Without whom this book would not be possible.

~

Most of this book is probably true

Acknowledgements

This book would not have been possible without my daughter Isabella, who saved my life, and Robert Kirkman, who may have saved my sanity.

Contents

A Stroke of Luck

The word stroke tends to stop people cold. I can see their brains skid sideways on it. I say, "I had a stroke." There's a panic filled pause… what's the appropriate response? They say, "Not, not a *real* stroke?" Understandably, they assume I exaggerate. "I almost had a stroke" is a common phrase, living in the same hyperbolic world as "I almost had a heart attack" and the excruciating over application of "epic." Ah, well, yes, an honest to goodness stroke. Or, if they are a medical professional or know someone who has had a stroke, they instruct me, "You mean you had a TIA" followed by the inevitable "not a *real* stroke."

Nope, not a TIA, I had a stroke, a real stroke, an actual stroke. A TIA would have been cooler, and not just because it means no permanent brain damage. A TIA means Trans Ischemic Attack. Being under attack makes me sound tough, whereas my CVA just makes me sound clumsy. It was a Cerebrovascular *Accident.* As in, oops, there went a piece of my brain! Where did I put that? It's actually *Acute* Cerebrovascular Accident, because there are attractive brains and unattractive brains, and mine is adorable.

There's no way to ease into saying you've had a stroke. Leading with "I'm fine, but I had a stroke…" helps matters, but only a little.

"I had a stroke." There it is, like an invitation to look for exactly how I've been incapacitated. New acquaintances do a mental run down of every weird thing I've said to them since we've met. Old acquaintances don't bother, because the list is too long. They stare at me, perhaps looking for a telltale droop to one side of my face. Or perhaps they are waiting for the punch line, the end of the sentence – "I had a stroke- of genius…" after all, who has a stroke in their mid-forties? Isn't that an old person problem?

We'll get into age-ism later. For now, let's agree that there are many words that are better than stroke. There are even more that are worse, but why tempt fate? Words that are better include lots of foody words (like chocolate- but only if you say it with a French accent) and sexy words (like silhouette), and then of course, anything actually spoken in French and most things related to sex. No insult to my Italian heritage, but there is something about that mumbling blended together casually intense French. Lingue. Forces you to lean in close and try to read their lips, Oui? Ironically, the mushy mumbling of words is a classic sign of stroke…Merd… Curses, of course, speak for themselves in all languages, with excellent consonants to crunch on (after all, who doesn't like a good 'Fuck.'). And there are outstanding, big idea words like bliss, freedom, joy, tenderness, delight, peace, followed by phrases of note— 'cracking up,' 'laughing your ass off'. Imagine it – a world where we can laugh our asses off! Big butt trends not withstanding, I would totally be behind that. The only possible improvement on successfully laughing your ass off is to 'die laughing.' I defy you to find a better way to go.

But, alas, I am stuck with the word stroke. I could toss around Acute Cerebrovascular Accident; giving me much needed time to myself while my friends stare at me blankly. Rarely does the conversation go all the way to "Yes, there is some dead brain matter in my head, just a spot of dead tissue, thanks." Who wants to think about that? That would be like writing a book about being brain dead.

Halting conversations notwithstanding, word of a stroke travels fast, particularly if you have an Italian mom. Emails and cards from my mother's circle of friends arrived post haste. Likewise cards from the children of my mother's friends and cards from the divorced partners of the children of my mother's friends. Including the males. You know the poop is flying through the fan when the male species is saying to you - out loud and in writing – 'hey, glad to hear you are doing OK.' Yes, that's a gross generalization, and all my west coast friends are now properly peeved. How sexist of me! I would apologize, but I recently had a stroke and I ____ (fill in your own excuse).

You'd think the medical pros that worked with me would be able to hide their surprise a little better. Their universal response: "You're too young to have a stroke." Why thank you. That's incredibly reassuring to hear, as you prepare to draw blood to find out if I am hyper coagulate. Good thing I'm too young to be in here. That ought to go over well with my insurance. You know what would have been helpful? If someone had just notified my brain about this age issue, say sometime before 8:25 a.m. on March 25th? Saved myself a lot of trouble and anxiety, I need someone to complain to stat-

My doctor says the blood thinners may give me some memory issues. She also said I could experience memory loss. And there was one other thing she said about the meds, but I don't recall what it was.

Ahem. But What the Hell Happened?

Oh right. Glad you asked. Forgot what we were doing here for a minute. Let me walk you through the luckiest day of my life. Or as I like to call it, Tuesday.

8:25 a.m. A small group of crappy blood cells decide to get together. They clump and bumble indiscriminately, very likely dumb ass their way into the wrong atria of my heart, and shoot up to my brain. After they muck around and interrupt my very large thoughts, the game is afoot. Ahead? A-head. The game is on…

My legs feel strangely lightweight from the knees down. Almost as if they are floating. I can feel them, they aren't numb, but they definitely ain't right. I give myself a moment to let it pass, and when it doesn't, I carefully walk away from the stovetop, leaving my turkey bacon behind – criminal. I think it burned. Come to think of it, I don't know that I ever turned off the skillet. It could be burning still…

My body has never felt like this before. Ever. The possibility of a heart attack intrudes. I know that symptoms for women having a heart attack are not the commonly known ones. Perhaps floating knees is among them? I need to get some adult help here ASAP. My neighbor is a police officer, maybe he is home.

I am able to walk over and sit down at the table. I will tell my daughter that if something happens to me, she is to bang on the neighbors' door and then call 911. Unfortunately, my brain and my tongue are no longer on speaking terms, so neither am I. This is what my brain tells my mouth to say:

"Knock on Ben's door. Tell him I need him. We have to call 911. Something is wrong."

This is what my mouth says instead:

"Frind ged nian."

That is not right. Hmm… perhaps I should try again.

"Dogerran nid."

Now come on. That's just absurd. That's not even a word. I'm a bad improv actor faking a language. Let's do this one more time.

"Frngah. Di ni gan- ger."

Tripping over your tongue is a misnomer- tripping is defined as light and easy movement. My words stumble off my tongue, barely becoming air born before smashing together on the floor, scrambled beyond meaning. Someone has combined and re-arranged the syllables and it's extremely annoying. My eight year old looks at me and giggles, because suddenly Mommy is so very bad at speaking. I say it perfectly in my mind, carefully fix it in my head, yet my tongue throws a tantrum each time, and it takes a moment to realize that it didn't come out right. Again.

I wait. And then wait again, to be sure. Slowly I try, slowly I speak. Two words should work. By now the look on her face tells me concern has replaced amusement.

"Get. Ben."

Ben is not home. Wait. Breathe. Think. Speak. I say, "Need. To. Call. 911." It comes out the way I planned, excellent news. Ah, welcome back tongue!

I run a checklist before everything I do – before I speak, I consider what the words are supposed to sound like. Before I move, I consider exactly what I want my body to do. The pre-planning is necessary so I can do a post mortem on every single tiny event – did my leg move? Did my tongue agree with my brain? What is next? Lungs, ears and eyes seem to be doing OK on their own which is good, because I have very limited mental space right now and I don't know how to make any of those very important things happen on demand.

My daughter brings the phone over. What are the steps in dialing my phone? Press the button that looks like a phone. Then 9, 1, 1. Because my phone is smart, smarter than I am at this point, it asks me if I'm sure I want to make an emergency call? Do people in emergencies really have time to confirm this? After some convincing, my phone finally agrees to make the call. The timing of all this is delicate– I don't know how long I have before brain and tongue disconnect again. I'm not sure if I outwitted my phone or the technology gods took mercy on us, but it connects to a dispatcher.

I'm speaking slowly, but clearly. My daughter is at my elbow to help. The dispatcher asks everything you'd expect, and we are told to stay on the line while we get a new dispatcher on board.

Between the first and second dispatcher, I notice that my hands are shaking – another symptom? My brain tells them to stop, and they do. Good. Basic motor control. I may perchance have a bit of extra adrenalin running about. Or several gallons.

My daughter is amazing. She never cries, never panics, just goes about doing what needs to be done. She pays very close attention to the dispatchers at 911, following their instructions precisely - she secures the dog, unlocks the front door and occupies her toddler brother.

My brain and my mouth seem completely compatible again, but I'm treading lightly, unsure when they'll disagree. Not the kind of thing one normally considers – thinking before you speak is a rarity for almost everyone (for further proof: see social media); never mind waiting long enough to see if there's still a connection between your brain and your tongue.

The EMTs and police arrive to the cacophony of my irate dog, secure in her crate and certain that these strangers in odd attire are here to do us harm. I talk them through the symptoms. I'm asked to get a neighbor there for the kids pronto, which I'm able to do.

"Hi. Everything's fine, but could you come down here? I need to go to the hospital."

She arrives and I stand up to walk myself to the door. Which I am able to do. I know I am walking slowly, but I've no idea how slowly or how strangely until much, much later, when my friend tells me the EMT asked if that's how I always walk. I don't hear the question, if I had, I could have told them no. I am typically as graceful as a ballerina in a pas de deux, as long as I'm wearing proper footwear. In improper footwear I've been known to fall off the side of a road, flip over, roll for quite a while and land sideways in a prickly bush (I actually have this on video somewhere. I was holding the camera. It's thrilling footage). I make it to the ambulance without incident. I am walking out of my house, leaving my children behind. Now what?

Alone with my thoughts, the ambulance ride is quiet. There's nothing to do but wait, and think, and listen to the siren. I know something very very bad has happened, I suspect a stroke, what else could tangle my tongue that way? My speech wasn't slurred though, the classic stroke symptom. Instead, my brain invented and simultaneously translated my words into an entirely new language. In four seconds. No one said the word out loud, and I didn't dare say it in front of my daughter. I have no way of knowing that my incident was called in to the hospital as a "near fainting," this in spite of the fact that I never used the word faint except to say, "No, I don't feel at all faint, no dizziness, no, no fainting." Now I'm just waiting for the professionals to work this out. It will be a long wait.

The ER is surprisingly busy on this Tuesday morning given that it is neither a full moon, a Saturday night, nor some combination thereof.

The triage nurse, a hospital's version of a concierge, greets me at the entry to the Emergency Room like I've arrived for the brunch special: "So how are you today? What can we do for you? In both legs? Uh huh. Your speech? OK. And how do you feel now? Do you take any medications?"

Just a multi-vitamin.

She is as blasé as the gatekeeper at a five star restaurant, while scanning for every possible symptom of every possible illness. I pass the velvet rope test and my traveling chaise rolls to a luxuriously appointed curtained area, known as Room #26. I know what you're thinking. Damn. She got 26? They must have really liked her. Before jealousy sets in, let me assure you, I was told within moments of arriving that the ER really was in need of renovations. Exactly what you want to hear as you put your life into someone's hands and machinery.

"OK, right in here. The nurse will be right with you. This place has really gone to shit. We need to renovate the whole place. Or at least get some curtains."

"Hi, how are you? Doing OK? Sorry about the cramped space. We really need a renovation here; I hope the money comes through. We just need more space."

In the fantastic repetition exercise in redundancy that is checking into a hospital, I get to tell my story to at least four people.

My attending nurse: "I'll be your nurse this morning, how are you today? And then what happened? Anything else? Your speech? Any numbness? No? Nothing numb? No? OK. I'm just taking your blood pressure. Oh, do you take any medications?

Just a multi-vitamin.

The nurse who took blood, followed by the nurse who attached an IV of solution presumably to replace the fluid just taken, followed by the nurse who attached me to my first set of heart monitors. I haven't seen this many separate factions trying to work together since I directed by first opera.

"Oh, do you take any medications?"
"Oh, do you take any medications?"
"Oh, do you take any medications?"

Just a multi-vitamin. For good measure I stop someone in the hall and let them know I take a multivitamin. Got to get that in the chart, dammit.

I'm hooked up to various things that beep, ping and sigh. That's correct. Way beyond the machine that goes bing. Medicine has improved a lot since a bunch of Brits delivered what might have been a baby. A nurse (take your pick) praises my excellent veins, which I've heard before when donating blood. I may have missed my calling as a heroin addict, though I hear that's a brief line of work.

The parade begins. First up, Dr. ER. He's sandy haired, bespectacled, and incredibly calm the way people who function in highly stressful situations have to be. Every employee in the ER, in fact, reminds me of nothing less than outrageously well-spoken sleepwalkers, for the utter lack of panic among them. But then again, they are under the impression that I'm here because I "almost fainted."

I tell my story (seventh time? Eighth?) and by now I'm quite good at it. I run down my symptoms, both legs, my speech (which has entirely returned), no faintness, no dizziness, nothing prior, no issues, no history, no smoking, no nothing nada nada nada zilch. No reason to be here except for that small incident where my brain stopped working. Just that minor annoyance. What else was I doing on a Tuesday morning?

We go through it all again with a fine tooth comb, pushing a baker's dozen of repetitions. Any sensitivity now? Anything on either side of my face? I seriously consider this inquiry. How is my face? I realize I've never asked this question of myself, reserving it for pre-dinner fishing for compliments and post-dinner, 'honey do I have spinach in my teeth' check-ups from my husband.

How is my face? I won't pretend I don't know my face – I've seen it quite often over the years while occasionally brushing my teeth, and yes, I've watched as Mother Nature turned it into a line drawing. But how is my face?

Face? Any thoughts? I am suddenly aware that I'm aware of my left cheek. I have no other way to describe it. Normally, unless part of my skin is touching something, my clothing, an armrest, whatever, I'm not aware of the edges of it. But my left cheek – I can feel where it meets the air. "Is it numb?" I consider, then, "No. I'm just aware of it." I'm painstakingly precise in how I answer all their questions. I won't agree to it unless it's the exact right word. I'm not sure if it's the writer in me or because I lost my words that morning, but I'm not going to let the wrong word suffice. "OK. I'm going to go look over your chart, and I'll be back." And he disappears behind curtain number one. OK then. I'll be sitting here, looking fantastic in a scarf made of medical tubing draped dramatically over one arm.

While Dr. ER and I have been chatting, a nurse added a number of punctures to my body, as well as several sticky bits, needles, bandages, and several things on wheels that have cords and lines disappearing under my gown in various places. Between the bed itself and the apparatus, I'm a traffic jam, and this is not a big space. They really need to renovate.

Lovely Hubby arrives and time restarts. Relief and release. He can be in charge for a bit. I allow myself to tear up. For some reason, the moment someone else can be in charge, I collapse just a little, a slight slump in relief that immediately affects my tear ducts. There's really no time for that. I remember to breathe after I get over my moment of weeps, and Lovely Hubby tells me about the music that came on the radio as he raced to the hospital.

"*Love Vigilantes*. By New Order?"

I reward him with a blank stare. I love music, I just have no idea who sings what.

"I heard it and I thought, oh crap." It was a moan of despair.
"What's it about?"
"Oh, it's just this guy…this soldier, who goes home to his family and realizes that he's actually… never mind. I also heard *The Stroke*."

I crack a smile. We chat. I fill him in; give him my story. Thirteenth time? Fourteenth? Dr. ER returns. "Well. Collectively, these symptoms could be a few things. So we'll run some tests. You're very young for a stroke and it doesn't usually present this way. It could be very very early signs of MS. We'll do an MRI to see what's going on."

What's left of my brain took a quick tour of Multiple Sclerosis and what that nightmare might mean, and immediately shoved it away. Was I going to look back on that moment making turkey bacon as the first moment I felt MS? Fuck no. That is not happening.

"Oh, do you take any medications?" My machine sighs for me. Just a multi-vitamin.

An MRI:
The Interactive Portion of the Book

If you've never had an MRI, please attempt the following to experience it fully (the following experiment could be dangerous and may lead to injury, death, or worse, so never ever try it). First, get a large, metal trashcan and a big plastic bottle. Depending on the size of your noggin, your head might fit in a one gallon, or may need a five-gallon. I think a three-gallon would be just about perfect for the average adult, based on the studies that I did not conduct and never fully imagined.

Follow these steps carefully (never follow these steps):

1) Put your head into the plastic jug (you may need to cut a hole. Have another adult help you with the really sharp knife, after all, you just had a stroke.
2) Keep the knife nearby (you'll wish you had it when you get to step ten).
3) Have the other adult pretend to be the MRI tech and say repeatedly, you have to lie still. Lie as still as you can so we don't have to repeat the test. Lie still. OK, don't move. Please lie still. When you have reached your absolute limit of listening to this instruction, repeat it forty more times.
4) Repeat step 3. Twice.
5) Request classical music to be played to calm you. I asked for something I could dance to. She just smiled and said, lie still.
6) Have the other adult remind you again to lie still. Try to understand – you just had a stroke, you can't be expected to remember these things.

7) What am I supposed to do again?
8) Have the other adult turn the music on at your neighbors' house, to simulate how you will not be able to hear it when your headphone plug comes out of the jack.
9) Lie (still) with your body inside the trashcan and your head inside the plastic jug inside the trashcan. Once settled, do not move. Other less creative writers would refer to this as lying still. Don't be fooled.
10) As you lie, still, waiting for the process to start, think about early episodes of *The Walking Dead.* Consider that you are trapped inside what is essentially a large tube with an opening that is just big enough for the undead to reach in and grab at your ankles. Consider briefly what it would be like to be eaten from the feet up, while your head is trapped in a plastic case so your neck is being stretched to the limit while former medical personnel gnaw on your Achilles. Or worse, your shinbone, and you know that would suck, because banging your shin on something is unholy painful, so a full set of teeth working on it would be agony. HA! I can fool the zombies by pulling my legs into the machine – which won't be a problem by then because the technician was eaten and really, who cares about MRI results when the Zombie Apocalypse is ON!! I have no idea how to actually escape the machine or the room, which has only one door, but I'm willing to bet the ceiling is drop ceiling tile type set up and I can get out through an air duct. Isn't it comforting when you pre-determine your Zombie Escape Route? Really, could there be a better sign of mental health?
11) Here's the real solution – Zombies, as everyone knows, are attracted by noise, and so far this is a relatively quiet- OH MY GOD WHAT IS THAT GODAWFUL RACKET?
12) Back to our experiment, so you can fully appreciate the volume involved in an MRI: Give some hammers to some toddlers (never give a hammer to a toddler) and allow them to bang on the trash can part of the pretend MRI contraption until your skull explodes (toddlers are natural born Zombie Killers, by the way) I don't recommend you allow them to bang on the plastic jug encasing your head, but then again I don't recommend this experiment. For further accuracy, allow them to throw rocks at the trashcan (never give a toddler a

rock). If you don't have rocks or hammers, golf clubs will also work.

13) By the way, you don't actually realize your head is in a plastic case until you stupidly open your eyes during a break between twenty-minute rounds in the machine and take a quick peek. Stupid, stupid girl. You have about an inch between your nose and the plastic helmet thing. When they ask 'do you have problems with claustrophobia' the correct answer is 'fuck yes.'
14) When the noise has sufficiently damaged your eardrums beyond the point of pain and you can no longer hear, the MRI is nearly finished. Just 19 minutes to go.

I enjoyed twenty minutes in that machine; followed by a two minute break during which I discovered my head was encased in a closely fitted plastic helmet, followed by another twenty-minute cycle. It really was that loud, and the plug on my headphones really did come undone (which I had no way of knowing). So the calming music was non-existent and the technicians' commentary, which I assume, was both encouraging and informative, could have been a recipe recital for all I knew. Having solved the Zombie Apocalypse scenario, (yes, I did envision a zombie situation and yes, I did work out my escape route) I had plenty of time leftover to focus on surviving a plain old MRI without having a nervous breakdown or developing a twitch.

So, how did I get through thirty plus minutes of deafening noise and potential anxiety enclosed in a tightly fitted plastic face helmet inside a metal tube? I counted. I counted the minutes. Literally. I counted to sixty seconds as slowly as I could, taking a long slow breath in between each second. And that was my focus. That's it. Numbers and breathing. A meditation can be anything, even a walk down a hall, as long as you stay focused on it. So with no other available solution - I really was afraid to let myself fully daydream lest I inadvertently jerk away from a chewing Zombie and ruin the test-

OK, hold on. Let's be honest for a moment, since we've got oodles of time before the end of this test. My Zombie daydream ending is going to involve Norman Reedus, because obviously he would be rescuing me and then in turn, you know, eventually I'd rescue him because I'm a Zombie Killing Badass but of course we'd never get together because who has time for that in the Zombie Apocalypse (note to self: make the time) and oh crap, I think my hand just moved as I thought about reaching for my cross bow… Did I twitch? Did I ruin it? I might have, because Charlie Brown's teacher just stepped in for the technician and mumbled something at me over the intercom, but it's tough to decipher because she's drunk and underwater.

As I was saying, my ability to focus was a real lifesaver. It's a testament to my highly evolved meditative abilities that I only reached five minutes when my first round was up. Or maybe counting slowly was all my brain was capable of at that point. I asked my brain, but it was trying to reach an air duct in the ceiling by standing on top of the MRI machine while Zombies gathered, so we'll have to get back to it later. Later as in after my brain escapes, finds shelter, and booby-traps the shelter for both humans and Zombies. You should note that the humans, of course, are the real problem in the Zombie Apocalypse. Honestly, when you find shelter, build a moat and fill it with Zombies. Don't make me spell this all out for you, my brain is tired.

Bad Good News, or a Stroke of Unluck

After a thrill ride of an MRI, I am returned by my chariot driver to the calm and quiet of my luxury suite in the soon to be renovated ER to await the results. It doesn't take long (always either a good sign or a very bad sign, like a trial, a quick answer is never neutral).

My MRI is good news in that we've identified the problem, but bad news in that it includes dead brain matter. Harumph. It's strange. When your good news is bad news, it gets very complicated for the docs. What is the appropriate tone? Good news! We have an answer – part of your brain died- Yippeeeeeeeeeeeeeeeee. The cheering and bit of dancing dies down in embarrassment. Actually, it was good news, given that my symptoms were essentially already gone and we didn't have to go any further down the 'hey there's a super off chance that this could be early Multiple Sclerosis' road. I'm still in denial on that one.

So, Dr. ER comes in, says, well, you had a stroke. Lovely Hubby looks a little shocked (who is this old lady he married?) but honestly, I knew it when it was happening. I just wasn't going to say it in front of my daughter. In complete honesty, I think when he said the diagnosis I said, 'oh shit' out loud, but Lovely Hubby swears I didn't. So there it was. 'Now, of course, we need to find out why a 44 year old had a stroke.' That's OK, you identified the problem, and everything else will work out. "Oh, and you have to back into the MRI for an MRA."

Oh shit.

So I won't just be skipping out of here today. Really wish I had gotten to eat some of that turkey bacon. We will now refer to our previous experiment – however, before entering the tomb of insanity, I did mention to the technician, hey, you know, I couldn't actually hear you while I was in there. 'Oh, the headset must have come undone.' Problem identified, problem solved.

And truly– problem solved! This time I could hear the classical music. Which reminded me of a medical procedural I was formerly obsessed with called *House.* Said cases nearly always involve an MRI. When the victim of the week is in the MRI, incredibly horrific things happen – like their eyes start to bulge out, or they hallucinate about Zombies, or they find that their partner has been exposing them to metal poisoning, so it starts to leech out. Through their skin. Ripping it to shreds. Good stuff.

An MRA is way more fun, because it feels exactly like an MRI, except your veins and arteries are injected with god knows what so they can see them on screen. Safe to say it's a liquid that isn't generally supposed to be there, otherwise they wouldn't need to put it in, would they?

By the by, if you are unfamiliar with *House*, a brilliant doctor solves cases, *but he was really grumpy about it.* I'm simplifying, but not much. Of course, *he* was played by Hugh Laurie and well he's Hugh Laurie. Do I really need to explain? Seriously, the final three episodes are brilliant, and reveal a level of friendship between two characters that I don't ever recall on screen. So refreshing. Not a 'hey bro' or an action sequence anywhere to be found. Unless you count a plugged, overflowing toilet plunging from an upper floor into an MRI, destroying the machine and potentially smushing someone. Yup, a toilet slamming into an MRI could have killed some poor schmuck. Dead in an MRI. Thank God I only thought of that just now.

Upon my second exit from the can of crazy, I've lost status, and I am unceremoniously parked in front of the curtained area that used to be my room. Oh, how I long for that thin veil of privacy, where Lovely Hubby and I could freely discuss all manner of obscene things, with nary a thought to our eavesdropping neighbors. Oh, how much more vulnerable am I, as I sit in my bed in the hallway.

You know, they ought to renovate this place- they seem to need more rooms. Most of the rooms have curtains that are wide open, displaying a variety of patients in various levels of consciousness. Apparently once they figure out what's wrong with you, they like to show you off. "See? This is Kimberly. She killed some of her brain this morning, but we figured it out. We're going to park her right here to be a lesson to the rest of you – don't go thinking you can go have a stroke at an early age with no risk factors and we won't figure it out, because we will, we will tangle you up in machines, and we will figure it out. Oh, and we're going to dress you poorly while we do it. Consider yourselves warned."

I look around a room full of people experiencing perhaps the most vulnerable moments of their lives in full view of not just the strangers helping us, but other strangers with their own life or death issues. We're a gallery of sculptures conceived by a madman and dressed by my old Italian aunts – blue housecoats for everybody!! And the kicker is, nobody minds. If you fix me, I will wear my blue housecoat and my octopus of medical tubes and sticky bits and I will sit in a hallway with my ass hanging out if need be. Just. Fix. Me.

I don't have long to reflect on the ghoul gallery because among the bells, whistles and beeps of modern medicine a good old fashioned alarm bell sounds. "Sounds' is being modest, it shrieks. Almost immediately after our return.

Oh crap. We are right back in the middle of the Zombie Apocalypse. That's right, Lovely Hubby steps out of my room (or rather, walks away down the hall) to take two seconds to pee and over the speaker I hear, "Code Red in the MRI suite. Code Red in the MRI suite." Followed by that intermittent, extraordinarily loud buzzing that can only accompany bad news. Oh my god, CODE RED, that must be the zombie code, that nice tech is probably trying to eat a patient right now – pulling on some helpless patients legs and ripping the flesh off while her head is trapped - nope. Hubby returns to inform me that there's a fire in the MRI suite. Sweet mother of god. Who had to sit in the tomb of insanity during that? Truth be told, they probably didn't even hear the alarm over the friggin' racket that thing makes. He confesses that he too was planning an escape route, as the bell was remarkably similar to alarms one expects to hear during the Zombie Apocalypse. His escape plan, however, did not include me, as I am now apparently a liability. Thank you, loving husband. Don't let me slow you down, Shane.

Feeling magnanimous, I decide to assist Hubby with his escape plans, as I will obviously have the luxury of time. Hubby and I spend the better part of 20 minutes working out our escape route, potential weapons, and which are likely to be the toughest zombies to kill of all the potential zombies walking around. There are some seriously strong medical assistants running about who could do some damage. But they don't worry me. To me, it's the quiet ones. The ones that haven't made a peep since we got here, are barely alive as it is, and then they'll suddenly be re-animated, and they're sitting right behind you and –

I'm convinced I can make a weapon out of my IV stand. I'm sure it comes apart, and there's bound to be a sharp point on one end or the other. Hubby disagrees. I can tell he's already left me behind in my weakened state. Fool! I'm a perfect pet- part Zombie, still me.

The real tragedy is that I'm in no position to test my own Zombie survival theories. Here's one for you – if the zombies are the all you can eat buffet type (not limiting their fare to brains but feasting on flesh all over) the solution requires some preparation, but is still quite simple. Follow me here—if you just put a plastic bag over those fuckers' heads, they can't eat you. They'll just wander around gnawing at the inside of the bag – I don't think they have the brainpower to reach up and rip it off. Hubby disagrees, but it really doesn't matter, because when I left the house in the ambulance I neglected to bring a box of Ziplocs. And he doesn't deserve my brilliant plan anyway, seeing as he already shoved open the revolving door and headed for the van.

And right there, right then – I come to the sweet realization that I am, in fact, a superior being, Zombie Apocalypse wise. My summer camp archery experience not withstanding, I have a distinct advantage. *I am already a zombie.* Or, at least, a partial zombie. A part Zombie. A half-time Zombie. No, that sounds like the undead running on the field at a football game.

Regardless of what we call it, part of my brain is dead, and therefore not nearly as appetizing as the rest of you whole, freshly brained people. Ha! Don't be jealous. We can't all be brain dead. Who would the zombies eat?

That's some good bad news, that is.

I Love a Parade

As I'm already in the hallway, I'm in a prime position for the patient parade (note to the staff – even if the patient is not within earshot, the other patients all know who you are talking about, particularly if you insist on discussing the difficulty of lifting someone). I'm in 'room' 26B. That's right. The deluxe part of the hall. My section is extra busy. If you weren't jealous of my brain dead-ness, go ahead and be jealous of my accommodations. It comes with all kinds of entertainment, in the form of overheard conversations and medical diagnoses, as well as other patient sculptures to gaze at and play "what's she got?"

I am quite certain that no one is going to guess "stroke" when looking at me. Hubby and I take several fun trips to the bathroom, which includes getting a nurse to unhook me from the octopus apparatus, walking on my own (hold your applause), doing my business (good dog!) and heading back. If you need to take a moment here to slow down from the fast pace of this book, I understand. No need to risk a stroke.

When the parade of doctors starts, however, it gets really fun – and it's all for me! I get a visit from Dr. Drive-By, Dr. NeuroKnows, Dr. Attending, and a few who aren't actually looking for me. I tried to accommodate those last few by throwing out symptoms I think they might be looking for, but I sense that's not helpful and their real patients are waiting. Ruining my fun.

I feel like an unwilling member of a relay race, in which doctors are released one at a time to run at me, ask a series of questions 90% of which are required to be the same as questions the other doctors ask. They are permitted a brief pause to reassure me and then run off again to tag the next doc.

Allow me to briefly introduce you to Dr. NeuroKnows. He's a bit younger than I am, the tie, the coat, the inevitable flipping through of the charts. He asks me details about the stroke itself, both legs, my speech, etc. I don't remember much about our initial conversation, it wasn't particularly engaging or witty, but that's fine. I don't want a date; I want him to fix my brain. Alas, my initial reticence eventually proved correct. He would not be the one to fix me.

Dr. Happy Attending stops by, and a few other very helpful people, none of whom were particularly good entertainment, and let's face it, I was in limbo waiting to see what we'd test next, so I was really looking for something interesting. No one has said a word about food, and we're working on 4pm now. I am heading towards twenty-four hours of unintentional fasting; so unspeakably foreign to me it seems impossible.

And suddenly, he appeared. Dr. Drive-By. I figure out that he's there for me before he does, given his purposeful stride and clear lack of understanding of the ER layout. He seems perplexed by the array of patients displayed for him, and confused by our gathering in the hallway. Maybe he can suggest some renovations.

I took a good look at him as he flew back and forth. He wore a tie and a nice smile (he had on other clothes, I'm fairly certain, but I remember the tie and the smile). Walking around an emergency room in a tie and a button down shirt instead of scrubs speaks very loudly, and here's what it says: "I do not deal with blood, vomit, or other bodily excretions. I'm here to talk with you." Or at you, as it turns out.

I look at him hopefully every time he zips by. I don't care if he's a doctor of mine or not, I'm just looking for a break in the monotony and he seems like a happy puppy. It's been twenty minutes or several hours since the alarm bell went off, and there hasn't been a code red or any other color. For entertainment value, this ER is turning out to be a bust… He finally circled in on me, slowing down his stride and curving back like a German Shepherd about to nap. Around and around… and around… and around until- no, one more circle—and… down. Good boy! He cruises to a stop bedside, and correctly identifies me. That's the last thing I'm certain he said. I cannot stress how fast this gent was talking. I take no responsibility for accurately recording any of the following, because he talked so fucking fast. And I'm from Boston, so I know fast fuckahs, a'ight?

Raceyoutothebottomofthepage, andgo!

"OK,
All right,
So what happened this morning?
Any fainting
Were you speaking
So not words but sounds?
Words? Not words-
Combinations of syllables?
Mixed?
And comprehension?
Yes and responses were-
Uh huh
And the sounds were-
Syllables and they-
Uh huh
And your leg both legs
And how long did that last
Dizziness-
No? No? None? Not?
And the speech returned-
Sentences or-
And the words were right or-
And that was when-
You felt it was-
Did you know-
And you said-
And what you were saying-
And how long -
No?
Oh, yes?
Then…"

I suspect I am somehow being tested – he's talking so fast I don't have time to think, which seems a bit cruel considering a piece of my brain just died. Is he here to stress test the rest of it? When the stroke happened and I tried to speak, my words were crisply articulate and completely incomprehensible. I don't have time for these considerations, because the Q&A is approaching light speed.

"That's good-and how old are you-any history of anything like this-no-good-ever been hospitalized-do you smoke-and follow my finger-Drugs? And follow-look up-spell Chesapeake backwards-good-no-any prescriptions-any non-prescriptions-any descriptions-renditions-revisions-definitions-circumcisions-all right we're going to figure out what this was and make sure it doesn't happen again. OK?"

"I, forty-four, no, no no, no, OK, what? No, I don't think, that's, no. All right. OK. Um, who, who are - who were you?"

And he's gone. Whoever he was, I was reassured. Thrilled to hear that I will be well, and in fact, completely cured of whatever it is that we haven't yet figured out. None of that seemed to matter. The fact that he didn't introduce himself and disappeared in a puff of smoke notwithstanding, I felt better. He said the magic words – 'make sure this doesn't happen again.' So reassuring. Of course, he may or may not have been a doctor. He may or may not have been a random, bored person in a shirt and tie. I could very well be the hospital version of the idiot who gets a call and gives out her social security number. 'Hello? Yes, this is Kimberly. Yes, I have a social security number. Yes, I think it's secure. What? It was stolen? How did that happen? It could have been an Internet virus? You just need me to tell you the number so you can check it? OK. Can I give you my bank account passwords as well – could you check those? Everything is going to be all right? Oh, thank you, thank you!'

I'm probably not that dumb. And I don't think I gave him any information, but it's hard to say. I'll have to re-read that section. Come to find out, many moons later, while reading a copy of my medical report, he was the linguistics portion of my neurological assessment. Part of my neuro team, there to test my language and verbal skills, looking for 'diminishments.' Ironic, given his rapid fire delivery and the fact that he didn't pause to take a single breath in the course of our 3 minute and 47 second conversation. He was, however, grammatically perfect. Bravo.

Your takeaway: You'll probably have to request a copy of your medical report, like I did. Chart flipping is for professionals only.

ERE (Emergency Room Etiquette) or Stuff I Thought Everyone Knew

While we have a lull in the excitement (once they know what you have, they can take their time about why) let's have a look at some good general ER knowledge:

1) They are going to take care of the guy having a heart attack before you.
2) They are going to take care of the woman about to produce a new human by squeezing it out of an opening stretched beyond comprehension before you.
3) They are going to take care of that kid who is seconds from death because someone didn't realize that no peanuts also meant no peanut butter. Before you.
4) You can complain about 1, 2, and 3 but it won't matter.
5) If you are the patient and they are talking to you, you are in good shape. If you are with the patient, and the staff is talking to them and talking to you, your loved one is doing OK. If at any point they stop talking to you, or if they walk in but don't talk to you and immediately start pounding, cutting, hammering, stretching, squeezing, or stabbing the patient with needles, etc. – there's a

problem. Be glad you are in the ER and back away.

6) Don't argue with the nurses. Really, that's all. These people know what they are doing. If you don't think they do, then do everyone a favor and don't go to the ER for assistance. It's your right to bleed to death in the road if you wish (I believe the Zombies refer to that as a roadside diner).

All that whining I did earlier about having to tell my story hundreds of times? There's a medical reason for that. The questioning, not the whining.

On a previous trip to the ER— not one of my dumb ass ones, one of the other ones that weren't my fault. Well, OK, the car accident was technically my fault, but it wasn't my fault I was driving. And it wasn't my fault I was pregnant for sure. OK, that's wrong, it was at least half my fault I was pregnant. And I don't mean fault I mean responsibility. So, yeah, OK, it was my fault I was in the ER. But by the time you finish this book you'll realize why I can say this was my fault, but not because— OK, fine. This was another brain dead moment that landed me in the ER. It just doesn't make my top 3. Or my top 10. Can you just stop asking about this? Thanks. So, given my earlier complaints about the repetitive nature of the redundant questioning system in an ER, I'd like to revisit and offer this more objective explanation. I'll use some overheard conversations, and being clever, I think you'll glean the gist of all those questions.

An older, let's say 50's gentlemen sits in the next bed. I know he's a gent for sure because the nurses and orderlies call him sir occasionally. Other than that, he's hidden behind a curtain, as am I. Affording the perfect way to eavesdrop. As a writer, I should just travel with a curtain. People will say anything on the other side of a curtain. For further proof, see any Catholic confessional. I assume he's older, based on the gravel content of his voice; it's possible I'm wrong. Let's call him Lenny. Lenny was asked the Question Series repeatedly for an hour, by different people. Apparently, he made regular appearances in the ER (the docs reading this are already diagnosing some of his issues) but lacked my charm, as they were pretty abrupt with him. But then again, he was having a heart issue, so maybe they didn't have time to be chatty. The dialogue went like this, and mind you, these conversations are no more than two minutes apart, maybe three, max:

Round One:
"I see you are back with us."
"Yeah, it's my heart."
(Tubes, monitors, machines that twang are being attached.)
"Your heart is bothering you? What does it feel like?"
"Pressure."
"How old are you?"
"53." (BINGO!)
"OK. Did you have breakfast?"
"No."
"Did you have alcohol?"
"No."
"Did you have medication?"
"No. Yes. No. No medication."

Round Two:
"I see you are back with us."
"Yeah, it's my heart. You know."
"Did you have breakfast?"
"Yes. A bagel."
"Did you have alcohol?"
"No, no alcohol."
"Did you have medication?"
"No."

Round Three:
"Did you have breakfast?"
"Yes. No. I didn't eat."
"Did you have alcohol this morning?"
"No."
"Did you have medication?"
"Angina? What's the med called?"
"Aspirin?"
"Yes, an aspirin."

Round Four:
"No, I didn't have anything to eat this morning."
"Yes, I had a beer. And an aspirin."

Round Five:
"I took an aspirin with a couple of beers."

Round Six:
"Yes, I had breakfast."
"What was breakfast?"
"A six-pack. I had a six-pack, around 11 a.m."

I was glad there was no Round Seven. I'm not sure I could bear finding out he'd downed a six-pack, a jug of moonshine and a squirrel. Lucky dude. What if they had taught him all the way?[1] Apparently patients are like Termites – don't trust them. And definitely don't join them for breakfast.

As referred to elsewhere, this is not my first ER trip. In fact, I've been to this particular ER four times in less than three years. Twice for me, and twice because I have children and that's what they do. I know good ER etiquette. For example, from a trip to a different ER in the beautiful city of San Francisco, a word of advice I longed to give to my ER roommate. We can call him the asshole behind curtain number two.

Ahem. To the Asshole Behind Curtain Number Two:

If you are that idiot guy, who put a ladder on a hill, and then fell off of that ladder when it fell over, and broke your ankle when you fell and hurt your head when the ladder landed on you, let me share with you advice you will surely ignore when you repeat said stupidity in the future (I can call him stupid, because I confess my own stupidity elsewhere, which makes me therefore holier than thou and immune to criticism. And now I stick out my tongue at you.) Where were we? Ah, yes, stupid people and how they turn their denial into blame on others.

Dear Sir Who Broke His Foot in the Dumbest Way Possible,

First, don't swear at the nurses. These are the people who control your pain meds. These are the people who speed up the visit from the doctor. These are the people who will either do a great job wiping your ass when needed or leave you with monkey butt.

---

[1] Lost? Don't worry. It's not a stroke. It's just a television reference I warned you about in the disclaimers.

Second, know that you are an idiot. Acknowledge your idiotness. Embrace it. Laugh about it. Charm goes a long way to cover stupid [for further proof: see any election prior to 2016].

Third, give up control. You are in an ER. You need help. As Dr. Friend once told me, "if you're in an ER and you aren't having a heart attack or a baby, you did something dumb." Sir Broken Foot Bone - you broke a part of your body that isn't even supposed to bend. So if the nice nurses need to cut off your "fucking new leather boot" that cost you "200 fucking dollars" to get to the broken ankle, let 'em dumb ass.

Oh, and put on the "fucking johnnie." Nobody gives a shit if you look uncool. You fell off a ladder you placed on a hill and then it fell on top of you. You are not cool.

ERVE (Emergency Room Visitor Etiquette)
or Shit I Thought Strangers Knew

On the flip side of this, and on a completely different ER occasion, I offer this advice to that super sweet lady who asked me while I was in transition labor if I was having twins because "WOW" I was "HUGE- so HUGE".

Ahem. To the Dear Woman Who Has No Idea How Close She Was to Death:

Don't ever say anything to a woman in labor. Ever. No- no- don't argue- shhh…not ever. Your silence could keep you alive. If you must speak, like, you have some medical disease that prevents you from keeping your mouth shut, or you're Italian, then just say, "you are beautiful" or "you are amazing". But truthfully, it's best to be very quiet. Shhh… And avert your eyes. Thank you. The life you save may be your own.

Oh, and if you are unfamiliar, 'transition labor' is when your cervix goes from about 8cm to roughly the size of the Lincoln Tunnel, or 10cm. Some women are able to blissfully remain polite during this period of excruciating pain. That's fucked up. If you'd like to experience this without pregnancy, labor, delivery, and the ensuing lifetime of parental obligation, stretch your nostril until you can push a grapefruit up it as you do super slow squats with a gorilla on your back while you have to poop worse than you can possibly imagine, but the poop is blocked by someone's head and body trying to tear it's way out of your groin. That's 8cm. Bump it up 319% for 10.

Where were we? Ah yes, the emergency room. I'm feeling good enough to feel grouchy about not being given anything to eat. Seriously. I'm one of the brain dead over here, people. Get some chow headed my way or I will take matters into my own hands. Finally, they've not only decided to move me to an actual room in the hospital, they are actually going to do it! Like right now! You read that correctly. Right now! Note: The time span between a member of hospital staff telling you something is going to happen and said thing happening is long enough for new symptoms to appear. Au revoir curtain walls!

Lovely Hubby goes off to rescue the neighbors from our children, before I am officially checked into my new room. It's only been a short nine or ten hours since my stroke, and look at all the fun we've had. Hubby says he'll find me when he returns with the kids. I'll make it easy. My room will have a gurney blocking the door from the outside.

The Stroke of Midnight

Francesca has been living by herself, in a little house about an hour drive from her nearest relative. She's my roommate because she fell and broke her hip. I imagine she was much kinder to the ER nurses than Sir Broken Foot, given that she hasn't made a peep. And then I realize, it's because she is asleep. When she wakes, she's disoriented; she keeps asking her son where she is? I think perhaps a little bit deaf as well; he's increasing his volume with each repetition. Maybe he's just frustrated, but I don't think so. He seems… resigned. She drifts in and out of her nap, so I hear this conversation over and over again. 'You're OK, mom. You're in the hospital; you broke your hip. You're all right.'

Her confusion is echoed on my side of our curtain by the hospital staff as they visit me for the first time. The quick flicker in the eyes of each nurse- they look up from my chart, glance at me, and look right back down to check my age. I'm too young for the cardiac floor. What am I doing on the cardiac floor? Glad you asked. Because they have no physical evidence that my stroke was caused by a hemorrhage or aneurysm, it's classified as cryptogenic. However, it is possible that there's a hole in my heart that allowed the clot through. More on that later. Meanwhile, I'm up with the old folks on the fourth floor, because if my body waited 44 years to cause problems, it can wait another 12 hours to start figuring them out.

My eavesdropping is assisted by Francesca's confusion – she asks for details of her life not typically explained in such detail. Discussion with her daughter-in-law reveals that her son flew in from overseas. The decision has been made for her; she will have to be in an assisted living home. It's a disheartening preview of later life, and I wonder if she knows. She was a music teacher, violin; her students will have to be notified. I think she must be an incredible teacher, given that she is still teaching at her age. It's easy to think warm fuzzy thoughts while we're still awake.

When my young ones arrive around 7pm, Francesca panics, pulling at the curtain, who is it? Who's there? Her son quickly reassures her and explains, again, where she is. I imagine my son's little voice is particularly confusing.

Meanwhile, on my side of the fence, my toddler delightedly climbs into bed with me, my medical apparatus octopus will not deter him. 'Hi Mama, I like your bed' and he snuggles right in.

My girl is a little slower, looking at me intently, looking for a sign, I think, that everything is OK. After all, the last time she saw me I was jumbling up syllables and carefully walking around, like, well, like a zombie while she managed to get me help, get her brother situated, and take care of it all. Everything is OK. I thank her (how can I ever thank her?). She is incredible. And very, very quiet. I will be OK. We know what happened and we'll figure out how to fix it. And no, it won't happen again. I get some more kisses and hugs before they have to head home to bed; after all, it's a school night. I am amazed at this new normal, kiss Mama goodnight in the hospital, head home with Dad. It's an excellent dose of Vitamin Love before I head into a very long night. I don't dwell on how I got there, I'm already focused on how to get out and get home.

Misdirected Anger?
What the Fuck Do You Mean by That?

It's 2 a.m. and Francesca is snoring like a jackhammer – I can't believe she's getting any oxygen to her brain at all. I briefly consider homicide. OK, not briefly. I consider ways, means, and excuses. Really. If they don't want the patients to kill each other, they should provide earplugs. That probably sounds harsh but I want to heal my brain. I need to heal my brain. After all, it's my brain. I need it and it needs sleep. Then I realize I'm the only one on the floor who still has full hearing. No wonder no one is complaining about the lack of earplugs.

Although I know far more than I should about her, my roommate and I have not officially met, so I feel the tiniest bit rude plotting her death. Frankly I don't think the hospital pillow is thick enough to smother someone. At least not fully before help arrives. And we're all attached to monitors, so help would probably come pretty fast. I must really need to get some sleep – I'm so rarely homicidal.

At this time I'd like to extend an extra friendly thank you to the super awesome nursing assistant who suggested to the deaf woman in the next bed that she turn on her TV at 11 p.m., because between snores she is somehow changing the channel. While she sleeps. Perhaps she swallowed the remote and I am listening to her choke on it. Which seems sad, given that she's actually a nice person when I'm sound asleep. There's nothing I can do but go for help – earplugs.

I lie there working my heart rate up in a simmering rage, talking myself in and out of taking action until I finally bounced from the bed, johnnie flapping, heart monitor octopus pinging off the charts. I storm the nurses' desk. I am cause for alarm – a patient out of bed, without assistance, looking really fucking grumpy. Given the hour and the fact that they have more information about me than I do, I skip introductions, "EAR PLUGS. EAR PLUGS. NOW NOW NOW!"

Luckily, I do not spy the super friendly nursing assistant of loud television fame. Apparently she turned on the tube and skipped town, trying to avoid the wrath of the crazy young coot in Room 3008. The scramble begins, "Oh, we're out, we don't, we don't have, let me see, I don't think I, we don't really have…" several nurses are searching and fumbling in the enormous desk, trying to appease the crazy lady.

"NO- UNACCEPTABLE. IT IS 2AM. I HAVE NOT SLEPT. I. NEED. Earplugs." This last slides off into a whimper. Silent prayers ensue. I've stopped talking but my entire body vibrates with exhaustion. They find me earplugs.

I pledge undying devotion and bolt back to bed. I can storm around like this because I am still wearing the pajama pants I had on when I had my stroke. They're bright red, and my hospital gown floats out behind me, giving me a whimsical crazed cardinal vibe. I'm so tired. And I stink. Reek. Bad. Like wandering around Georgia for months in the same clothes. Who cares. I'll ask Lovely Hubby to bring me a sleep mask tomorrow and with the earplugs to boot it will be like staying in the worst hotel ever. A hotel where you are not allowed to shower. A hotel where they constantly tell you rest, while constantly waking you to perform vampiric functions.

I wake up on day two (good dog!) bright and early with a nurse of some sort needing a fluid of some sort. At least he's handsome, and I oblige as best I can.

While I'm waiting for my next visitor, Francesca is marched by me to go off to some procedure, I assume (how or why they have someone walk who has a broken hip is too much for me to figure out). She's tiny. I could tuck her under my arm like a football. How did all that noise come out of such a small body? I realize the combination of size and power probably makes her a terrifying and terrific teacher. It's like looking at a lion in the body of a sparrow. She pauses on her son's arm and looks me dead in the face, "Ah. The other victim."

Dammit. Great line. I can add professional jealousy to the list of reasons to kill her. I think we would have gotten along well if I didn't want her dead when she snores.

After a bit of breakfast I am wheeled for an echocardiogram. I am instructed to lie on my side – not that far- and put my hand up – not that way – and then sort of lean – just a bit – to be in the exact right position – now hold it, right there- while indescribably disgusting goop is spread over my heart. I am thankful that my head is not encased in plastic. Like all hospital tests, the technician is not allowed to reveal what they see, as it might be construed as an 'official' diagnosis. She tells me everything looks good.

On the way back to my room, I'm mulling that over. It's good that everything looks good, but it's bad if that means that my heart doesn't have a hole. Because where did the clot come from? Not that I want a hole in my heart. But I definitely don't want more questions. My musing is interrupted by a comment as I pass by. Again, hospital staff, just because someone is on the cardiac floor, it doesn't mean that she's lost her hearing. Someone in scrubs is staring at me as we wheel by. She bumps her chin in my direction and offers this to her buddy, "I feel so bad for her." I assume she's talking about the dread lock that has begun to form on the back of my head. No showering is allowed while wearing the heart monitor – oh yeah, combine that with the various gels, adhesives, bandages, and sticky circles of hell they use to keep an eye on things and my skin is a nicely simmering stew of yuck. I prefer to assume she's talking about my dreadlock than about my premier status as the youngest stroke patient on the block. That's right – minor celebrity on the cardiac floor. I attack the dreadlock back in my room. It's a project that will take the better part of the afternoon. I work with a tiny black plastic comb given to me in my welcome to the ward kit; the likes of which hasn't been seen since grease was a word.

Dr. Cardio stops by for a chat. She's young, sharp, simultaneously fantastic and unpretentious. The echocardiogram wasn't conclusive, so tomorrow we'll do a TEE (Trans Esophageal Echocardiogram). There's a tube, there are pictures, we'll be able to see if you have a PFO (Patent Foramen Ovale). We are looking for the mysterious hole in my heart. Apparently, my ribs are in the way during an echocardiogram, so we're going down the esophagus to get a look from behind. Sounds cool.

I left my ability to tell time somewhere. Nor do I know what day it is. I arrived on a Tuesday, so weekday is assumed. It feels like I've been in here for at least three days, but it's possible it's only Wednesday. Life at home is going along without me—unfortunately I didn't even think to suggest a note explaining the circumstances to my daughter's teacher. Well done me. Her teacher's concern was understandable- she queried my daughter about her absence and got the chipper reply, 'Oh, I was at the hospital. My mom had a stroke.'

The standard response ensued: “A stroke? A real stroke?” Yes. A real one.

Exit the Body Factory

Early morning on day three I barely have time to run in and pee before my ride shows up. I am gurneyed down a thousand hallways. I find myself constantly saying 'excuse me, sorry, excuse me' to people, as if the gurney is really my gigantic ass that's getting in the way of everyone. Like it's my fault I'm so cumbersome.

We rumble into the ambulatory procedure lab/place/motel, skidding into my 8x10 foot space surrounded by the ubiquitous curtains. Thank goodness for the curtains, I might have forgotten I was in a hospital. My curtain opens not only to the room like everyone else's, but also directly to a double set of glass doors leading to a very busy hallway. As much fun as I'm having people watching, I really don't want strangers checking out my… procedures. So to speak.

No matter, a nurse earns my love with a minor miracle. A warm blanket. Literally, it has been warmed up. Who thought of this? Pardon me while I moan in relief. My god, a warm blanket feels so damn good in a hospital. I didn't even know I was chilly until my bones started to thaw. There's a special place in heaven for the blanket warming angels.

I give my name rank and serial number so often I begin to wonder if I'm not actually part of a larger experiment, and answer every 'how are you' with, 'how are *you?*' Really, we know I'm a mess or I wouldn't be lying half naked on a portable bed waiting for someone to shove a few tubes down my throat and take some snap shots of my potentially broken heart. We know I'm in some sort of sucky condition. So really, how are *you*?

I am hyper self-conscious of the fact that I didn't get to brush my teeth before they loaded me up, and pity the person who has to actually put the tube down my throat.

Dr. Cardio enters. She informs me that she rechecked my echo and that my heart is, and I quote, "pristine." I assume she's talking mechanics, as I've certainly had dark moments and my share of heartbreak. Not to mention the road rage. Still, it's a great word. Pristine. Pristine. Pristine…untouched. Cold. Like an ice queen. Oh crap. That's not good. Untouched? As in my heart hasn't been touched? What does that say about me? Wait, what is she saying? Ah, the PFO. If they find it, they can fix it. Such good news. Such good good news. Fix it. Make it go away. I'll be better before I walk out the door.

I play another round of the "but who are you really because you might have changed places with someone in the 7 seconds since we last asked you" game. I apologize for my now lethal breath. Nerves are not good for halitosis. But I'll be asleep for all that. An anesthesiologist (we'll call her Dr. Hair because of her absolutely kickin' do) runs through her checklist of questions, including a mega list of drugs they want to make sure I haven't ingested lately. I'd like to pretend that up on the cardio floor the biddies and me are doing nothing but party after lights out, but it's not happening. So no, Dr. Hair, no pot, no cocaine, no heroin, no – I don't even know what that drug is. Is Dr. Hair just tossing street names at me in the hopes of tripping me up? I am sorely tempted to say wait- yeah I do that. Whatever that purple thing was that you said. Who am I kidding? I can't even pretend to pretend to take pretend drugs. The list is so damn long that her tone actually changes about halfway through it, and it starts to sound like an invitation. Wait, are you offering or- no- of course not. I haven't done any of that shit, but really, shouldn't I get to ask all of you all of that?

Where's the patients list of questions, just, you know, quid pro quo? Did everyone have their morning coffee? Nobody's angry with his or her partner or the dude who always takes their parking spot? No minor annoyances, right? Just making sure nobody pissed in your cornflakes and the bored kid at the coffee shop got your cup o' joe right. Want to make sure you're all happy happy happy and focused focused focused. Let's work this out before my ability to breathe is in your hands. You all like each other and get along? Anyone grumpy? Anyone out of sorts? Anyone need to pee? Truly, did anyone survey your drug intake? Because I'm about to let you put me under. Three deep breaths? OK, but I wasn't finished with… One, two,… I don't think this is gonna work…

There's a Hole in My Heart, Dear Liza Dear Liza

I wake up to Dr. Cardio's very pleasant smile and the utterly unshocking news that they found a PFO. Great. Now I have to actually learn what the hell that means. So, you essentially have a hole in your heart, and we can repair it. I'll send Dr. Fix-It to speak to you; he is the one who does the procedures. The only other thing to worry about is if you are hyper coagulate. Meaning that your body may just be overcompensating, you may be naturally clotty. We'll get you tested, just to be sure of course. But in the meantime, we'll go ahead with this.

Dr. Cardio warned, "Now, I need you to understand that you will be on some pretty heave duty blood thinners, and that your treatment may involve giving yourself injections of such and such."

"No worries." She looks at me. I reassure her that it will not be an issue. "Listen," I bragged, "I gave birth naturally. I can handle giving myself a shot." She laughed and told me how amazing I am. I brag further – it was a water birth. Yup, my son is a merman. She is appropriately impressed (really, could her bedside manner be better?). She tells me I'm meant to live a long, long time. I am so impressed with myself I agree. Idiot.

Medical assistant number 473 of this 3-day stay takes me back to my room, and very kindly walks with me to my bed. Hospital rules. They want to make sure I don't fall down and bust my head after I broke my brain on my own. I'm thankful I don't have to try and find my way around this place. I don't know how my husband, who is so skilled in so many ways, finds his way to my room each day. He has less than no sense of direction. Point of fact, he can't correctly point to the driveway while standing in the kitchen. I wonder briefly if the stroke killed what little sense of direction I possess myself. I imagine Hubby and I, driving around town, unable to find our way home when I finally get discharged. At least now I'll have a legitimate excuse.

Back in my bed and facing at least another day in here, I realize I should have taken the window seat when Francesca headed off to her new world. I write an absurdly long email to my out of state family because it's exhausting to repeat myself, explaining about the PFO and Dr. FixIt, scheduled to come by soon. I jot down a quick list of questions to ask about the procedure:

1) Will there be cake?
2) How long has the procedure been around?
3) How many of these has he done?
4) And what the hell is it again?

I am distracted from the cake question by the arrival of my own lunch. It took a significant portion of my day to decide on food for each meal. After all, these are really the only decisions I make while in here. I'm not allowed to choose my roommate, my attire, my sleep schedule, my activities, and on occasion, what I get to pee into. Perhaps this is why people complain so very much about the food in a hospital. It's the only thing we get to select, so it better be worth it. Lasagna, salad and chocolate pudding for dessert. I don't recall the last time I had pudding. I ate it of course. It's something to do for 19 seconds.

I Skype with my folks and my sister, several time zones away. Three little frownie faces looking seriously at me out of my computer screen. They seem worried about something. I wish I had an emoticon of a head with an exploding brain to send them. It might lighten things up. At least things progressed on my end that there is information to share. The hole in my heart may, or may not have been responsible for the stroke.

Dr. FixIt's arrival ends our chat, and he launched into the pre-approved elevator pitch on the procedure. PFO closures have been done for about 15 years (not true); he did about 1000 of them (I suspect also bullshit). Is this the reassuring number they tell you to use in medical school? I am vaguely reminded of a real estate person telling me what my house can sell for. No, no. Not 1000. Too perfect. Too round a number. No one has done 1000 of these. Dr. FixIt clearly indicates that he cannot advise me on whether or not to have the procedure, as he has an obvious bias about it, and then talks about the risks. I am deeply concerned by the now recurring phrase "the first stroke". The "first" stroke? The first one? How about the only stroke? Can we go with the only stroke? Just 'a' stroke. One. One stroke. Uno. Un. No need to go on, no sequels, just the one, thank you. I revise my earlier statement: The hole in my heart may, or may not have been responsible for the stroke, and may, or may not lead to future strokes because having one stroke immediately increases your chances of having another stroke.

I inform Dr. FixIt the phrase "the first stroke" is making me very uncomfortable. Like, a sharp pencil puncturing the buttocks uncomfortable. Or hiding in a trunk while a herd of Zombies strolls by uncomfortable. Small space, but definitely not a cozy time. He hightails it while I am still working out my metaphors. I guess once I said I was in, he was out of there. I sense Dr. FixIt may have commitment issues.

No matter, there's a new parade starting. The PFO repair nurse-assistant-tech-volunteer parade. It's really the only thing on, and I have a front row seat.

I'm given a pill, a powerful blood thinner. Powerful as in, don't cut yourself shaving if you don't have a lot of towels handy. Because of this dandy new drug, I also get a visit from a nutritionist, to discuss in detail the amount of spinach and kale I consume on a given day. I'm sorry, what? I'm expected to have this information readily available. Apparently, in addition to a shot at the remake of Popeye, consuming large amounts of these veggies, particularly kale, will mess with my system and Vitamin K levels, which could, in turn, mess with my ability to coagulate. Or not coagulate. Or something. Because as everyone knows, Vitamin K plays a role in coagulation. As in the German word Koagulation. Huh. The point being, this is carte blanche to skip on the super green veggies. The five year old in me is ecstatic, but the grown-up in me has developed a taste for kale. So it's an all or nothing proposition. Eat the same amount every day while on the drug, or not at all. Seriously? Seriously. Huh. Well, a typical day means I have difficulty remembering to eat a regular meal, never mind a regular portion of a regular veggie. I don't foresee this working out well. I'm given literature (pamphlet, booklet, essay and article), menus, small print information, a bumper sticker, several lapel pins, a pen that writes in kale green ink and I'm pre-registered for the Kale Eaters Anonymous 5k Fun Run. Got it. But we should in no way be concerned about pharmaceutical companies' over involvement in our medical system. It's totally fine.

I settle in for the night – earplugs in. Apparently I will miss my daughter's science fair after all. They need to observe me while I'm initially on the super duper blood thinner drug, just to make sure. Make sure my blood thins, make sure it doesn't thin too much, it's not clear what we're making sure of, but we want to be absolutely certain. As always, I'm happy to stay if there are unanswered questions. I'll do this drug therapy stuff; and then we work out the PFO repair surgery. Good. Sorted. We have a plan. But wait! You thought that back fence was secure, but no no no. Someone left it open and the undead are squishing themselves through. Remember, it's walls, then a fence, then a moat, then another fence, then a line of cars, and then some other stuff. Never stop working on the perimeter. Ever.

Dr. Neuro-Knows breaches the room in a rush, waving some papers and telling me that no, I don't need surgery, all I need is aspirin, because there's no point in surgery, it doesn't improve my odds and "Isn't that great?" He took my horrified silence for acceptance and understanding.

Wait. What just happened? There's a hole in my heart. And we're going to fix it with… aspirin? Does my cardio know about this? Dr. NeuroKnows is still enthusiastic, "Oh, yes, I just discussed it with her and our attending and everyone is fine with it." The working parts of my brain suspect he is either new to the hospital, new to the team, or new to the profession. My silence screamed, "Really? Everyone is fine with it? Everyone? No one else comes to mind? Because I feel like someone was left out of the conversation, oh, now who could that be… hmm… let me think – oh wait, I can't think. Brain dead. If I could think I'm pretty sure I'd believe that I mattered in the conversation. Apparently not. What the hell do I care about my brain? After all, I've managed to kill part of it on my own."

Here, he tells me, I'll leave you the study (yippee more paper!) I've underlined the relevant parts (at first I assume this is because he thinks I'm a moron but when I do read the study I realize it's because most of it is bullshit that doesn't fit my case). Is he waiting for me to say "thank you!" Or "Here's a gold star, good job buddy!"? Big smile from the man in charge of my brain's health. "Isn't this great news? No surgery!"

Yeah, about that. See the surgery wasn't bad news; so not having it can't be great news. Please. Just. Wait. "Why aren't we fixing the hole in my heart?"

"Because there's no need. It's not causing a problem, so we can control the possibility of stroke with aspirin and it means no surgery. Surgery has its own risks and doesn't solve the problem; it has no proven efficacy.

Outstanding. So why do I have a sick feeling in my stomach for the first time since my stroke was actually occurring? Why do I suddenly feel unsettled? Let's review. I was fine. I had a stroke. I have a hole in my heart. But we don't have to fix it because it's not causing a problem. See, I feel like being in the hospital is a fucking problem. Like legs and language and brain not working = problem. All evidence to the contrary, I'm not here to pass the time.

Dr. NeuroKnows breezed out of my room with an oh so casual invite to coffee, or perhaps it was appointment reminder, "So I'll see you in a week in my office, then.

"Don't forget to take your aspirin. Oh, and here's the study to read over."

Hold, hold- hold up! "But what if I'm hyper coagulate? When my Factor V test comes back, what if I'm hyper coagulate?" Most of his body is already out the door as he pretends to pause.

"Oh, well then, sure, that's something different."

And he's gone. There's something enormously problematic about my current scenario but I just can't put my finger on it. My confidence in my care is crumbling…

I'm not sure how long I sat, trying to wrap my head around the fix it with aspirin prognosis. I understood it empirically, the aspirin thins my blood just enough to keep me healthy. Of course, I was in perfect health when I had the stroke. Lovely Hubby is home with the children, so I listened to the contradictions in care by myself. The takeaway for you: Have someone with you. Have someone with you just to hear the information you are hearing, and to ask questions.

Dr. Happy Attending sauntered in, floating on air, good news, right?

"Is everyone on board with this? I mean, did you have a conversation with my cardio about this?"
"Oh yes. The cardiologist, your neurologist, everyone is very clear. This is the way to go. I hadn't even heard of the research, but it is the latest information. Good thing he checked."

Yup. Good thing. Good thing he checked. Feeling really off about this. Of course, my two year old can pull up crap via Google on my phone but that doesn't make him a diagnostician.

"So, we'll get you out of here this afternoon, you'll see your cardiologist on Monday and neurologist in a week. OK?"
"Oh. K."

Explain to me again why we're letting all the zombies out of the quarry?

Getting discharged from a hospital takes a minimum of four to sixteen hours after whatever time the attending tells you you're going right home. Hospitals do not operate in the same time space continuum as the rest of us. They are in a specialized zone, called the hurry up and wait zone, in which you are either waiting for a procedure, hurrying to get to a procedure, waiting for a procedure to start, waiting to see if you've survived the procedure, waiting to see if your body functions after the procedure (proven by pee or poop more often than not), waiting for the results of a procedure, or waiting to be discharged right now. The only thing that happens right now is when you are woken up from a deep, nourishing sleep to take your medication right now, because it has to be that minute then. Otherwise the entire system falls apart. And back to our previously scheduled hospital discharge…

I am left with a prescription for over the counter aspirin, and if that wasn't confusing enough, a copy of a study I do not understand, and the disheartening realization that I have three days to get through before I can have a real conversation with my cardiologist. What the fuck. This stroke is no fun at all.

BUT- like a shotgun blast to the head of the zombie about to eat you - suddenly I got the amazing news that my girl earned second place for the second grade at the school science fair. If I can just survive long enough to get her into, through, and out of medical school, maybe she can change all this. Nevertheless, I am going home. I am still broken, but at least I'll be broken at home.

Or not. Before I can leave, I am stuck in a revolving door of questions between the education department and the marketing department. They are determined to wear down what little resistance I have left.

Ms. Patient Educator gave me an intoxicating speech titled "How To Know When You are Having a Stroke as Explained to a Person Who Has Already Had a Stroke". Or, the podcast version "These are the Symptoms that Made You Call 911, Do You Recognize Them?"

My silence quietly snarked. Huh. How about that? It's all so strange and new, lady, you're acting like I just had a stroke or something. So you're saying it's important to call 911? Slow down, woman. Can we review it again?

Patient Educator rapidly disseminates full color handouts to ease me into the explanation. I'm sure it was really useful information and it's a good thing that I have no idea where it is now. I was hoping for a working brain that I could mess with, but apparently we're only allotted the one. I review the beautiful description and detailed sparkly handout of stroke symptoms, none of which actually match what occurred to me during my stroke. I reassure her that I will be calling 911 in the event of anything remotely like a stroke. Or a hangnail. Or you know, a fart.

Patient Educator reiterates again (yes, it was that redundant) how important it is to get medical attention immediately.

"It's important to call 911 right away."
"I understand."
"Right away."
"Yes."
"Make sure you call. We have meds that can help with clots, but there's a time window in which they can be administered, so you know, get here quick."
"Got it."
"So, say you were having some symptoms, but you felt a little hungry?"
"Stop for a sandwich?
"No, no, that is exactly what you should not do. Don't do that. Don't stop for a sandwich."

"You're right, I don't particularly like sandwiches."

No, no, of course I didn't. But oh god how I wanted to. The temptation was enormous. What if the part that died is the part of me that's an asshole? Gasp – what if I'm perfect now? I wasn't at all snarky in fact I was extremely polite. It could be true. Having rid myself of my only fault, my general asshole-ness, perhaps I am now perfect.

What? Oh, she's still talking about what to do if I have a stroke. Why is she talking to me like I don't understand? I appreciate the effort; after all she has no way of knowing that I came in via ambulance. It's not like they put that kind of info in my chart. Which she is holding. On the page about admitting me. Where it indicates that we called 911 to get me here. If it was all spelled out like that for her, I might be suspicious that she was just going through the motions. The truth is, she's just trying to make sure I stay alive long enough to respond to my first request from the hospital for a donation (it takes a mere 6 days for that to arrive).

Sigh.

"Thank you. It's good info to have."

"Well, we just want to make sure you know what to look for. Don't hesitate to call."

"Thank you."

"Come back if you need to. It's important to get to a hospital."

Perhaps I look too happy to be going home, and she thinks I'm not taking her seriously. She's not the first to question if I understand my diagnosis. Yes, I get it. Part of my brain is dead. Yes, a piece of the brain tissue I started out with is no longer living. Not there. No connection. No signal. Radio silence. But here I am – walking and talking and thinking at least as rationally as I ever have – so where's the tragedy exactly? My buddies' mom had a stroke three weeks before I did and she was still hospitalized at that point. Point of fact, I found out that she was a smoker. They aren't kidding about that smoking shit either. Get your calcium; don't smoke. Avoid broken bones and broken brains. Your hip or a stroke, it's the kiss of death.

Inconvenient? Yes. But tragic? My stroke was neither calamitous nor disastrous. It could have been fatal, and therefore called lamentable, I suppose, if I'm in the mood to mourn brain cells. But potentially fatal and fatal are a lifetime apart, no? It certainly wasn't disastrous. In the event of an actual tragedy, I have prepared the following (I had hoped to make a video of this but I'm currently packing to move cross country, and really, who's going to buy a DVD of this book when my mom is the only person likely to buy the book, and she'll stop reading as soon as she sees the word fuck on page 2?).

Actual tragedies include things like:

Not realizing we already solved the energy crisis. It's called the sun.

Not realizing how lucky you are to be a parent, and that there are couples in the world that would give a limb, or several brain cells to be in your position.

Mistakenly thinking that your kids somehow asked to be here. You made them. Or you went to great lengths to get them. Don't turn around and bitch about it.

Thinking that the greatest tragedy in the world is two people who love each other and want to spend their lives together.

Anything my eight year old considers a tragedy, which can include worldwide issues and the fact that I inadvertently threw out that tiny little scrap of paper with a part of a word on it that might someday have been the greatest thing ever written, if it wasn't in fact lint.

A tragedy is thinking that your religion is the only religion and not realizing that to other religions, your religion is the 'crazy' talk.

The words, "I regret" are a tragedy.

Surviving a stroke with no issues? Not a tragedy. I'm feeling pretty smug about my imminent jailbreak, and I'm clearly feeling well enough to get back on my soapbox. I've even had time to wax philosophic, when my curtain is slung back and there she is - the Patient-Liaison-Assistant-to the Information-and-Education-Givers-Association-of-People-Who-Need-to-Talk-at-Me-Before-I-Can-Go arrives. You can shorten that to whatever you like. This job can also be described as "Well-It's-Nice-That-This-Person-Is-Gainfully-Employed-While-

Serving-No-Real-Purpose-In-A-Medical-Sense" or even shorter – "Marketing Research." She has a delightful survey for me.

"How has your stay in the hospital been?"
"Given that I am able to leave, brilliant!"
"Have you been well taken care of? Felt attended to? Felt safe?"
"Yuppity yup yup."

Although I cannot vouch for the safety of others if we're going to be doubling up without earplugs. I opt not to tell her of the homicidal state induced in me by bunking with a rip-roaring snorer. It could make me appear unstable.

And my personal favorite –

"Would I recommend this hospital to a friend?"

Fuck no. I recommend that all my friends stay really, really healthy. Hospitals are dangerous frickin' places full of god knows what kind of germs and deadly crap, and medicines administered by humans who can all make mistakes. No, no friggin' way.

Oopsie. I believe I may have messed up the marketing matrix. There's no room for reality on there. I should have told her – just advertise the warm blankets. The patients will come running.

I left Terminus with a much clearer understanding of how an assembly line works. But I left alive. Always the goal.

Your Brains, Your Brains, Protect Your Brains, Brains, Brains

It's day four, and apparently I walk around the house all day very distracted, pacing a marathon, not knowing exactly what to do. I'm gesturing and talking to myself for hours on end. Lovely Hubby thinks I may be worrying about things just a teensy bit but he's smart enough to let me wander. The sudden change in my medical plan has me twitchy and I don't know what to do with myself. My thought process is running counter clockwise and there's no next step. I'm stuck, and I need more information.

I have a call with my best friend from high school, an incredibly, brutally, beautifully blunt M.D. whom I trust implicitly. She is now head of a hospital and a host of other terribly impressive things that were entirely unforeseen when we were teens, discussing the men's soccer team for hours on end.

Despite seeing her daily from the age of thirteen to eighteen when we both went off to college, her opinion is still one I trust. And not because she's well respected and successful in her field. It's because she is, and always has been, exceptionally honest with me. I once read in a women's magazine that every woman needs to make sure she has one brutally honest friend in her group of friends. Apparently we also need one to drink with, one to sob with, one to celebrate with, one to shop with, and many additional activity specific buddies. Rather than start interviewing friends for positions in my posse, I stopped reading the magazine. My Dr. Friend is, as I said, brutally honest. And I love her for it. Come to think of it, pretty much everyone I consider a dear friend is really honest. Also, they all find me charming. They said so. Bottom line, if you can't trust the friend who as a teen offered to help you get birth control 'just in case' then who can you trust? Pre- or Post-Zombie apocalypse, she's an MD. She's handy.

We discussed the details of my case, and the two courses of treatment. She's objective and knowledgeable, and I'm lucky to know her. Aspirin vs. Fix-It run neck and neck, until we talk in detail about how the heart surgery will go. Cracking me open is wonky, bypass, obviously is risky, lots of ways for things to go wrong. Hang on doc - it's not open-heart surgery. They go in through an artery in my leg.

"Endoscopic?"
"Yes."

Ta-da! Things get simpler then. Dr. Friend's immediate take on my situation becomes "protect your brain" at all costs. After all, she reasons, you can actually live with your heart functioning at less than 100%, lots of people do (not that she's suggesting it mind you, don't go lopping off a ventricle or clogging your arteries with mud). But your brain? Protect your brain. Period.

She sounded like the opposite of the Zombie Mating Call. Come to think of it, you know those folks in the old movies where the Z's are super picky eaters and just chomp on brains? Well, why didn't the humans just wear helmets? How easy is that? I'm comforted that I now have survival scenarios for elitist brain eating zombies as well as general all-purpose flesh eating zombies. I don't share this with Dr. Friend. After all, she's a doc, and she's required by law to report stupidity. Or something like that.

Dr. Friend is kind enough to hunt down a neurologist for me (Dr. Sees-It-All) as an antidote to my current neurologist situation. She gives me a list of things to make sure the staff and hospital can handle if I go forward with the cardiac surgery (a what's what of stuff that can go wrong while I'm on the table) and a whole lot of questions to ask the neuros and the cardios. The list includes:

1) What interventions do they have in place in case the shit hits the fan while I'm under? The shit in this case being a clot and the fan being another part of my brain.

2) What if I don't do the surgery? What are the neurological implications for my brain if in fact I'm having microcosmic strokes for a long period of time?

> Also known as, what's the cumulative effect if my brain dies a little bit over a lot of years? I'm no doctor, but I'm fairly certain that this situation would be what we call "bad." Like forgetting to bring rocket launchers when you take the RV to the Hilltop.

And her general assessment – I'm probably young enough and healthy enough that if they break something or I break something while they're doing this procedure, more than likely it can be fixed.

See? Honest. Of course, in her best interest I now have to remind you that I had a stroke, and may very well have imaginary friends. Unless you think she's brilliant in which case she's totally real.

And then I get a little peak into her world. Dr. Friend sends me a host of articles and studies. I will summarize them here, to save you the trouble of ever reading a medical study article ever. This assessment is an accurate summary and reference for virtually any medical study ever done.

The article states that it will tell you two things:

1) What the study will prove
2) That the study, in fact, proved it**

And then proceed to negate all of that information by the following legalese:

** With relationship to item #2, the study proved efficacy within such and such a range of inaccuracy***

And will summarize as follows:

***Each case should be considered individually and none of this has any validity whatsoever should any aspect of anything deviate an iota from the described description unless certain circumstances occur in which case throw the whole friggin' thing out cause really, we're just making our best guess here.

Leaving room for a certain amount of interpretation on the doctor's part. I am amazed that anyone has the balls to practice medicine at all.

My assessment?

Medicine does not = Science.
Medicine = Art.

Chemists vs. Mechanics

To fix the heart, or not to fix the heart. That is the question. And the opposing teams are equally persuasive and mutually exclusive. Neuros Feng Shui your brain – but the furniture can't just be re-arranged. It's all chemistry and I don't like to mess with my chemistry set. "We'll give you this for that and balance the effects of it with this other thing and then counteract that with this" Wait, what was the original problem? And the cardios are at work on the human body – make it function! Make it work! Mechanics. Working on the most complex machine ever devised, but it's a very specific point of view. They have a lot of hammers. So they see a lot of nails. "Ooh! Yes! WE can fix that. We can chop off that piece and move it up there and re-attach those bits to these other thingies and Voila!" "Excuse me, doctor, the patient died ten minutes ago." "But her acne is gone!"

Let's play a little matching game, shall we? I'll give you descriptions of three waiting rooms, and you match them to the correct doctor: Dr. Sees-It-All, Dr. NeuroKnows, and Dr. Hockey. Which doctor goes with which room?

Waiting Room Number One: Almost impossible to find, as the information desk in the atrium lobby is unattended and no one in the other wing has ever heard of my doctor, I spend a full twenty minutes inside the building just trying to find it. Only to find out that I needed to go to the other waiting room first, the one on the other side of the atrium, in order to register first, of course. Of course. I don't dare ask where the bathroom is.

Waiting Room Number Two: Filled with toys, dollhouses and *Highlights Magazines* that have been rudely scribbled on with crayon (it bothered me as a child and it bothers me now. Look, we all want to solve the *Hidden Pictures* puzzles, so don't go outlining the pencil masquerading as an umbrella handle and ruin it for the rest of us). This waiting room has patients I could stack three high and still tower over. One little lovely is running down the hall in nothing but her princess unders, and that's fine. Because she's 2, and paper gowns are scratchy after all.

Waiting Room Number Three: Is empty. Completely empty. When you spend two hours plus with each patient, there's not a lot of overlap.

Don't worry, the answers will be obvious in a moment or two.

Part I Dr. NeuroKnows, or, What's Crazy About This?

I don't want to piss on anyone's parade, but not all doctors are good at being doctors. Just like not all teachers are good at being teachers, and not all cops are good at being cops. Sorry, but some of you made bad career choices. And we all get to comment on it because the jobs you do are so absurdly important. There's just no room for your bad career choice. Which brings me to my neurological appointment a week after I got out of the luxury hotel known as Local Hospital.

Having never been to a neurologist, or even so much as a therapist (like that's not obvious) I was so curious about his other patients. You know, the ones with the problems? Unfortunately, no one would meet my eye, and no one mumbled, and no one shouted obscenities. My daily walk to the bus stop in San Francisco offered a far greater array of issues to ponder. And not just because I lived off Union Square and culturally we like to pretend mental health issues don't exist, leaving little opportunity for healthy solutions and many opportunities for homelessness among the unwell. It was just slow going in the waiting room as I stared intently, on high alert for someone to do something, you know, *not normal.* Minutes ticked by. I was relentless in my intense observation. No one acknowledged my scrutiny. Or even my existence as I studied them. And bit-by-bit I realized they all became nervous and incrementally, the tension began to rise – who would it be? Who is going to flip out? What about that guy? 40's, heavy. Dark hair. Currently reading a magazine he brought. Germophobe? Hmm… I sneeze as loudly as I can. Nothing. I watch him intently for several minutes to see if I can see his heart rate go up.

The vein in his neck seems larger. Meanwhile the woman to my immediate right keeps shifting away from me in her seat, what's with that? She's obviously uncomfortable. Germophobe coughs. I spin to look at him…He's nervous. Seat shifter woman is uncomfortable too, she's flipping through her emails on her phone but way too fast for me to read them as I peer down at her lap…someone is going to lose it, and soon. Germ guy? Seat shifter? Ms. Basso? My name is called. I dutifully stand to leave the room and the entire place relaxes. Weird.

Dr. NeuroKnows calls me in, and I find myself in an office. See? Everything is so completely OK that I don't even need to see you in an exam room. I suppose that makes sense. No need for a paper gown to examine my brain. Or maybe all neurologists just meet in a room with nothing but a desk in it and two chairs. And no windows. And grey walls. With no art. And a desk void of personal objects. My concern for his mental health is growing.

We start with a review of my chart, and a hearty "How are you feeling? Everything back to normal?" I'm fairly certain that Dr. NeuroKnows has never had a major health event. I'm positive he's never had a stroke or been told there's a hole in his heart.

And the casual comment, "So, everything came back normal on your tests, oh, no, wait…" Extended silence as he perused something in my chart. Oh, I'm waiting. Believe me. On pins and fucking needles over here.

"Oh, you didn't have your Factor V test."
"Uh, yeah huh I did."
"You didn't."
"I did."
"Did not."
"Did so did so did so."
"No, there's no information here."
"I did, I called Dr. Happy Attending, who said that all my tests came back negative, including my Factor V test."
"No, there's no inclusion of that."
"It was done before I left the hospital, the blood was taken before I left the hospital, because the results take so long to get. We discussed it."
"No, the test was never sent."

What's left of my brain is really pissed off. My tests haven't all come back. Why was I told my tests *all* came back negative if they didn't *all* come back? This one is not on the neurologist. My relief that at least the error was caught had me thinking, OK, maybe we are on the same page.

The missing test revelation was immediately followed by his recommendation to cut my meds (aspirin) from 325 milligrams down to 81 milligrams, because really, everything is fine. For whom, exactly? I may actually be hyper coagulate since the test hasn't been done, so why are we cutting back on anything? My situation hasn't changed.

"OK? Feeling good? So you can get that Factor V test, it's just a blood test, but other than that, no need to worry."

My silence settled into a quiet chill. I was a child, eyes down, hearing things I didn't want to hear from someone I didn't want to see. In spite of my overwhelming desire to take my brain and run from his office, I had something else to bring up.

"Doc, during the stroke, I had symptoms in both my legs, and then my speech symptoms. Well, really language sypmtoms. So what does that mean? Multiple clots?"

He responded in a large complicated run-on sentence that I now share with you verbatim: "Well, there's a pathway in your arteries in your brain, mumbo jumbo, which branch in such a way, large words I assume you won't understand, that the effect can be essentially, veer off into an explanation of how a stork, or rather stroke works (but it may as well have been stork for the load of B.S. I was getting) and suchly and so forth and so on and that pathway can then branch in such a way at that moment as to render this purported explanation completely useless. I hope that's clear."

Internally, I mulled: Interesting, that's fascinating – you say if the blood vessels in the brain branch then the clot hits two places at the same time. Striking, considering that the control centers for movement and body awareness are in different regions from the language centers… Oooh! Here's an idea! How about you come clean and say you don't have a clue? Or, say yeah, there was probably more than one clot, but we can't know for certain.

He reminded me of teachers I've known, who thought they had to have all the answers. So afraid that their students would realize that they don't know it all. Nobody knows it all.

That's OK. He didn't admit to me that he doesn't know exactly why I had bi-lateral symptoms on top of symptoms in multiple areas, and I didn't share with him that I'm seeing other doctors. We wished each other well. I prayed his practice was not filled with stroke patients.

And now, just to prove that I clearly don't know it all, I must confess that his opinion about the repair is essentially the standard from neurologists. In retrospect I was happy to have it – if you are going to undergo surgery, it helps to have a naysayer on the team to force you to really think it through. But the explanation of my bilateral symptoms? Just explain it, dude. Not sure what all that other business was, but then again, I'm no doctor. I'm just a reasonably intelligent patient who had to become an overnight expert in her situation. So I'm not going to bother to call you on it. I don't have time. I have a life to get back to.

Don't worry. We won't see him again. I have been referred elsewhere. Your takeaway – keep asking questions until you understand the answers and they don't reek of cow poop.

Part Two: Let's Play!

I'm the oldest patient in the waiting room, possibly in the building. I take the high road and don't hog the Etch-A-Sketch. Or any of the cars. It takes a minute for the nurses to understand that I am the patient, not my two year old. I'm given paperwork, and dutifully fill it out right up until it asks if I'm potty trained, which I feel is a little personal. I return to the window and convince them to let me skip a few questions on the form.

It's exactly fourteen days after my stroke. We are in the office of 'The PFO guy', a pediatric cardiologist. I meet Dr. Hockey, so named because of the framed pro hockey jersey leaning against his office wall. Also, he tends towards hockey hair. I'm guessing he played. Or he still does. Given that he has an actual specific solution to fixing the hole in my heart, he can do whatever he wants to his hair. He is 'The PFO guy.'

Dr. Hockey's pitch is specific, full of easily understandable numbers, and delivered in the most matter of fact manner possible. He is the best of both worlds – the confidence of a surgeon without the arrogance. I'm convinced it's because he works in pediatrics. As in, if you're going to mess with my child's heart, you better know exactly what you're doing, and you better be able to explain it to a frantic mama and papa in terms they can understand in the middle of their distress. Oh, I get to talk to a pediatric cardiologist because most people become aware of their PFOs when they are young. Before they have a stroke.

He drew pretty pictures for Lovely Hubby and I, color-coding the parts of my heart and the blood flow in and out of my atria. He drew the wall between my left and right atria and explained that there wasn't literally a hole in my heart. The wall between these two vital pumps is actually made of two flaps, one from each direction. The flaps were supposed to close sometime before the age of two, making a nice strong wall. My heart was forty-two years overdue on construction. I despise tardiness. But there's more – not only was I late, my flaps were a mess. He treated us to a succession of pictures, illustrating my poor little flaps as they aged. By the time I had the stroke, it was just a wobbly mess. It looked less like a wall, and more like a bisected piece of overcooked spaghetti. Or the guts of any Zombie victim. Take your pick.

So this increasingly wobbly flap, located in an incredibly important organ, can open every now and again. And most of the time that's OK, as long as the blood flowed from left atrium to right atrium. Because the blood on the left side went to your lungs, where clots presumably get filtered and oxygen attained (again, no kidding about that no smoking business – why would you do anything to mess with the organs that help prevent strokes?) Anyway, when blood flows from right to left or 'upstream' so to speak, well, that's a problem. And should there also be a clot in that stream... well, then you have a stroke delivery system. Because your brain gets first dibs on your oxygentated blood. Like, instantaneous out of the heart, straight to the brain.

The numbers were also super fun to consider – one out of three people has a PFO. That ratio was down from one out of five from the first specialist I spoke with. Of the people with PFOs, less than twenty-five percent have a neurological event (unless it just happened, doctors don't refer to a stroke as a stroke or even a CVA. It's a neurological event. It makes your brain feel more popular). And of those people with a stroke or TIA, they usually aren't the people with a large PFO. Unless they are me. So I rolled the dice and came up short all over the place. Then again, not everyone can claim to have hosted a neurological event.

What's the solution to all of this? A pancake. A teeny, tiny pancake. No joke, the device is two very small, very flat disks, attached at their centers, like two pancakes stuck together with a piece of butter. It's small enough to be rolled and fed into a catheter. The catheter (tube) goes into an artery, all the way up to and into your heart. The device is thereby delivered. One half of the device is unrolled in your left atria, and tucked up against the problem area. Then the other half is unrolled on the other side. The remains of your sad and pathetic wall (or septum) are tucked into either side of the device, and the whole tiny package is left there. It's called a septal occluder. Eventually your heart builds up tissue over the device, and instead of a wobbly nasty wall you end up with a nice thick can't bust through it wall. Like the difference between a string with cans on it and a wall made of crushed cars. Also, the device is super cool and you are basically, bionic. Just saying.

And then we get to this part of the conversation, again: I can't tell you what to do, because you've only had the one stroke. If you had a second event, it wouldn't even be a question, everyone, neurologists included, say do the procedure. If you came to me, having found this PFO, but without a neurological event, I would not do the procedure. Because the PFO hadn't bothered you. My husband and I are done with neurological events. Sure, some of them are probably really spectacular and interesting. You know, in a real red carpet sort of way. But the last one we attended was called "Kimberly Had a Stroke On a Tuesday" and it sucked. No one wanted to be there, and the whole thing made me feel old.

There is less than no pressure in his pitch, and I find that disconcerting. Why won't someone tell us what to do? Oh, right. Because this was only "the first stroke." Upon leaving, I make an appointment to have the PFO repair surgery before I've even decided to have the PFO repair surgery. And that will be another six weeks to wait. You know you've found a good doctor when you can't get an appointment. I asked his office to go ahead and pencil me in for surgery, you know, just in case.

Part Three: Dr. Sees-It-All or Whew. That Was a Close One.

There is nothing malicious in his stare. This is not a Daryl squint nor Rick's sideways head cock lead with the eyebrow death march. Dr. Sees-It-All's face is millimeters from mine. Give or take eight inches. He stares. And he stares. And he stares. I am completely transfixed and exceptionally uncomfortable, but I couldn't tell you a thing about the details of his face. He had dark eyes, I do remember that. And his face had a general face-ness to it, nothing particularly extraordinary. Except for the fact that he didn't blink. I spent nearly two hours with this man, and he never blinked.

Even so, I can feel sweat trickling down my back. I wonder how long it's been. Maybe I should start counting, like in the MRI. I drift into a Daryl daydream and when I come back, he's still staring. Hopefully I didn't do anything super stupid like try to cut off an ear. So gross. Hunters need trophies but still. I bring my eyes back to his, and he's still looking. Not saying a word. I try to breathe without making a sound, because it seems rude to breathe loudly. I realize I've never been this close to another adults face for this long without a kiss being involved. OK. I forgot about the dentist. But he's not checking my teeth. He's staring. At. Me. The fact that my husband is sitting a few feet away makes it all the stranger. I am desperate to move but fear it will set us back to the beginning. I am definitely having MRI flashbacks. How utterly odd, considering that all this anxiety is caused by another person's face. Right. In. Front. Of. Mine. He's not speaking. I don't think he's breathing.

When I made the appointment, I had no idea I would be under such scrutiny. It took weeks to get in and I'm certain it was that fast because I'm too young to be a stroke patient, as we all know. His assistant became super helpful when she learned that not only had I already had a stroke, but I was also mere moments into my fourth decade. I have grown considerably older, however, since he started staring. I try to think of anything except the fact that he is looking at me… so uncomfortable… why won't he stop… Still. I am determined to keep still for this, desperate to prove my mental health. Maybe it's a trick. Maybe I was supposed to have already run screaming down the hallway "don't stare at me! Don't look at me! Noooooooooo!" I'm guessing not, so I stay put. Besides, the hallway and I are not exactly compatible, as I proved earlier in the appointment.

I already flunked walking, after all. It was my first test. We hadn't even gotten to the exam room, and he was already working me over.

> "Walk down to the third door and turn around and come back."

No problem. I've been walking for a while, like years. I can walk, I can skip, I can saunter, sashay, I can dance if I want to. I can leave my cares behind. Oh crap, what the hell shoes am I wearing today? Walk thirty feet, turn around and come back? P-shaw. That's nothin'.

"Oh, heel – toe, and walk naturally."

Of course. Of course walk naturally, because as every actor knows the easiest thing to do is to do something "naturally" after someone tells you to be "natural." I can walk heel/toe. I can. I just can't happen to do it in wedge sandals. Which I am wearing. Because doctor appointments count as grown up time, so I thought I would wear something other than sneakers. Yes, my life is so sad that a doctor appointment is "grown-up" time. You're just figuring out that my life is sad?

Anyway, I do my super un-natural natural walk, all the while thinking, "Do I swing my arms? Yeah, I swing my arms—swing 'em—NO! not that much—good—OK, walking, arms swinging just a little, heel/toe… heel/toe… am I walking too slowly? Is this slow or is this fast? Wait, too fast—too fast! Heel/toe… heel/toe…Toe/toe no heel… crap CRAP… heel/toe…nothing to see here just a woman casually walking the most natural way possible up and down a hallway while a doctor observes and her husband tries not to laugh… go about your business, please. I have this." I get back to the other end of the hallway without having fallen down or tripping over anyone or crashing into the various carts of medical equipment.

"Uh huh. Could you do it again without the shoes?"

Shit. Apparently I suck at walking. That much was clear. I was forewarned; this particular neurologist spends an inordinately long time with each patient. That's a good thing in my book; I like lots and lots of attention from the people who are taking care of my major organs. I just hadn't thought about how intense the scrutiny would be. He might be a neurologist, but he is acting like a mechanic. It's all observation of my physicality, with no room for saucy retorts. He's reading my brain through my body. I'm screwed.

And here we are back in the exam room, where he stares at my face. Still. I had time to consider if his exceptional interest in brains would make him a more discerning zombie. I also had time to realize that's an oxymoron. It's been 14 weeks, and I was just about to remind him that I have children who will eventually have birthdays that I should probably attend, when he sits back in his chair.

"Your left eye. The eyelid—"

My interruption rushes in to defend my face.

> "My eyelid has a little droop, yes, it's always been that way. Always. "

Lovely Hubby is completely baffled, bless him,.

> "Your eye does what?"
> "My left eyelid. It has a teeny droop."
> "No it doesn't."
> "It does. It always has."
> "I don't think so."
> "It does. I know it does. I'm the one who puts on my makeup."
> "You don't wear make-up."
> "True, but it is my face. I know my face."
> "I don't think so."
> "It does," from Dr. Sees-It-All settles it.

I was simultaneously thrilled that my husband never noticed the tiny asymmetry, and annoyed that I know they're asymmetrical. There's a reference to the cultural pressure to be perfect in here somewhere.

So this has been fun – a bad runway walk, a staring contest that ends in a listing of my face's imperfections, a marital squabble over less than nothing, and it's all a good way to relive junior high. Still, I was comforted by Dr. Sees-It-All's attentiveness. It's bizarre, and made more so by the fact that after each mini exam session with me he runs back to his office and apparently types all of this up in great detail. Still. He is "the stroke guy." His shiny lapel pin actually says "Ask me about TPA's".

Glad you asked. TPA's are meds they can give to break up clots, but there's a small, like two hour window in which they have to be administered. Ask your Local Hospital if they have them. As of this writing not everyone does.

Dr. Sees-It-All walked me through the events of the stroke in great detail, greater than any previous doctor, and I'm quite certain there won't be a single misquote in his report. After crawling through 90 minutes of examination (87 of which were the staring contest) we can finally just talk. When the recurring and terrifying phrase "the first stroke" comes up, it seems a perfect time to come clean. Lovely Hubby lays it out for him, "There's a hole in her heart. We can't see a reason not to fix it."

We know that he knows that we know the risks of surgery, etc., and he does not patronize us with bullshit. I lay it out the only way I can, "I hate the phrase the first stroke. I hate the implication of a second stroke. We don't get to pick where the next clot goes, or what it damages. I was just stupid lucky this time."

"We dodged a bullet," sums up Lovely Hubby.

I am delighted in Dr. Sees-It-All's response, non-committal as it may be:

> "I can't tell you that it would be wrong to have the surgery."

Holy crap, that's about as close to a ringing endorsement as I think I've heard. From anyone. He didn't tell me to do it, he didn't tell me not to, he didn't tell me that aspirin is my only course and the only thing I need. And yet. I ask him the one unanswered question that I still had:

> "Why did I have bilateral symptoms in my legs <u>and</u> speech symptoms?"
> "You probably had more than one neurological event going on at the same time."
> "So basically, multiple clots?"
> "Yes."
> "So, three areas affected, so likely three clots."
> "It's likely it was something like that, yes."

Thank you Boston – good night! That's all I needed. Every doctor on both sides of this argument spoke about my stroke as "the first stroke" or "the first neurological event." Well, it wasn't the "first" event; it wasn't the "only" event. I've already had three neurological events, count 'em, three: one (left leg), two (right leg) and three (language center) thank you very much, and it was all wrapped up in one decidedly fucked up morning. Nothing to do now but go back to Dr. Hockey and get in line.

Scared?

She is busy making breakfast, unaware that the entire world has changed. Overnight, an outbreak of Hollywood's best monster, the Zombie, took over her quiet little neighborhood. Her adorable children are in danger, she is in danger, the whole world is in danger. What does she do when the doorbell rings and the zombies arrive? Does she freak out, scream, freeze, back away slowly, or worse, back away quickly only to trip and fall 'damnit, how many times have I asked you to pick up your toys????' Does she respond in a panic, guaranteeing her evolution into breakfast? No, she picks up the butcher knife, or chopstick, or that fossilized carrot from the back of the fridge and stabs the traveling salesman zombie in the brain. Through his eye. Done. 'Kids, time for school.'

Unlike old Hollywood, I think the survivors of the Zombie Apocalypse will be moms. Nobody multitasks like Mom. Moms, look at your to-do list for today (it's that thing that has the 45 things you didn't get to do yesterday on it, along with a few unforeseen or ongoing items like "clean cat vomit" "find that missing miniature rocket booster" and "solve sibling rivalry"). Add "kill zombies" to it. Honestly, do you even notice the addition? Probably not, just incorporate that into your day, along with Zombie Kill Skills Training for your kids, competitive Zombie Attack Team practice, creating a new food source and finding safe water, and then go ahead with that "me time" that's so popular to talk about and pretend happens.

But Kimberly, were you scared? Have you been listening? No, I wasn't scared. Not even a little. I felt a lot of things – hesitation, anxiety, but actual fear? No. Not because I'm brave. (Stupidity and bravery are often confused. I tend to the former.) There wasn't any time. I simply didn't have the time to be scared. And more than that, I didn't have the luxury of being scared. Fear is a luxury sometimes; it means that someone else will take care of the problem. It means you can sit and worry a bit, oh no, oh no, this is bad, this is bad, that Woodbury kid just got eaten, someone is brunching on the dude in cellblock C. Back in the real world, Zombies roam freely in your living room, bumping into the new arm chair and smudging the walls you just cleaned-- oh come on for crying out loud! Or, if you're me, your body falls apart. I had to solve the issue and I was the only available grown-up. Things were dire. Like, Rail Car A dire - Rick stuck under the bed dire – let me introduce you to my friend Lucille dire - only it was just me and my kids alone at home. So no time for flop sweat fear.

I was home alone with symptoms that made no sense and were not decreasing. I could fix only one part of the scenario – I had to get someone else into the house so that if I lost consciousness my kids would be OK. I didn't know if my symptoms would get worse. I didn't know if I would lose consciousness. I didn't know if it was progressive, if it was a fluke. I didn't know much, except that something was very very wrong in my body.

The moment I spoke, or tried to speak, however, I knew it was a stroke. And the clock ticked faster. Would my speech come back? Would I be able to write down what I needed my daughter to do? Would I lose motor functions? My brain had two simultaneous thoughts: "Something is wrong" and "Make the kids safe." My children have to have a mom that is taking care of things, even when things are falling apart.

I have a favorite saying, usually when there's a lot of drama going on in the house over a lost shoe or hairbrush or some other really critical item like that little plastic thing we had that one time: Panicking never helps. Because when it really is time to panic, you simply don't have time to panic. When the unthinkable happens, you need to solve the problem. If you choose instead to run around mindlessly, you may as well be a zombie. Nothing is solved by screaming when the zombies arrive, except to call more zombies. I have yet to find a situation where this did not apply. Perhaps if zombies already surround you and screaming will alert Daryl as to your location, fine. But really, why would you leave Daryl's side?

Panicking never helps.

My Grumpy Vagina Contradicts Me

My vagina was grumpy. And not just because my husband was extremely concerned about having sex while I had a hole in my heart and it could, I guess, potentially blow up my brain if I really over-exerted myself. Yeah, did you catch that? I could literally have had mind-blowing sex. And like all trite sayings, be careful what you wish for because no good can come from those who wait to oh fuck. I had a really great mixed metaphor going there and it left the building. Blah blah blah I had a stroke. Oooh, I lost my train of thought. I have got to stop bullying me.

Where were we? Ah, yes, my vagina. Apparently day forty-seven was a good day for some high level panic, because my vagina decided, essentially, that tissue meant to be inside my body would have more fun outside my body, where it could be really painful and scare the piss out of me.

Granular tissue is the formal medical term, and as with all medical terms it is hugely misleading. The actual term should be:

> "Holy shit, honey what does this look like to you shit that hurts don't touch it is that blood is it bleeding I think it's bleeding oh my god I'm going online to see what it might be what the hell look at this picture what the hell IS THAT oh my god I should never have gone online fucking last thing before bed disaster"

tissue. From the Latin – Panicus Maximus. Which identification is followed by six, count 'em, six hours of hard core overnight prayer and deals with God, god, the Almighty, and all the mighty of his and/or her friends. That's right, I went polytheistic all over it covered every option, followed by a day of last minute appointments with my midwife and Dr. Super Gyno, also known as Dr. No Fuss No Muss.

Understand, this was actual tissue coming out of a gland in my body when it is supposed to be inside. *Inside my body.* So I am literally turning into a friggin' zombie at this point. Flesh falling off and the whole nine. Turns out though it was nothing, a slow healing area from a previous surgery. "Ha ha ha, did you think you had cancer?" said the mild mannered mid-wife. "Well, yes." (Hilarity ensues). Never mind, off to Dr. Super Gyno for the fixit.

Dr. Super Gyno is able to leap tall buildings of awkwardness, but more importantly, today he has a solution to the scary ass problem. And it's a doozy. Are you ready? Burn it. BURN my vagina. That's right, just a quick chemical cauterization of this bit of errant tissue and off we go. I use this little stick and- What the fuh-ha-ha? It's burning. Burning my vagina. Whisper it or shout it same horrible outcome. And the hands down best doctor response of all time to my involuntary exclamation-holy-crap-rat-fuck-pain gasp was-

"Does that sting a little?"

I was too busy trying to stay conscious and preventing my eyes from rolling back into my head to say much, so you can send me your own brilliantly snarky replies, much appreciated.

Where the hell was I? Ah, having a stroke. Hang on, I think I forgot to take my meds. The universe also chose this moment to lay my husband off of work. Which was super, it's not like we needed our medical insurance at the time. Panicking may not help, but sometimes it feels good to scream.

My Hero

Unlike myself, who couldn't have a stroke without squawking about it, my daughter didn't speak often about that day. So when she did, it wasn't easy. For her to do, or for me to watch.

Her head was bent low near the table, and her voice soft. A scramble of a ponytail tried to hold her hair back, but the strands fell across her face and almost hid her grey-green eyes. I couldn't help but stare as she spoke.

> "It was a Tuesday morning. My mom was making breakfast. I was sitting at the dining room table. She came over and sat down."

She paused while I restrained myself from putting my arms around her.

> "She tried to tell me that something was wrong, but she couldn't talk right. Her words were jumbled. Our neighbor was a policeman. When she could talk, my mom told me to knock on his door and tell him something was wrong. But he wasn't home. So we called 911."

It was the first time I ever heard her describe that morning in detail, and it was months and months afterward, at a Girl Scout meeting. Her new troop was earning the First Aid badge, and my girl was sharing her experience of calling 911. Ironic, of course, because she earned it with her previous troop and that practice is what made it easier for her to help me. She didn't tell them much more than that. She still doesn't discuss it in depth; she'd rather leave her part out of what happened that morning. She'd just rather not talk about it publicly. It's understandable. It can't be fun to watch your mom cease to function the way a person is supposed to.

The truth is, she laughed. She laughed when I tried to ask her to call 911 because it seemed like I was tripping over my words, and I couldn't stop tripping. She looked at me like I had lobsters coming out of my ears. And that's funny. It really is. Like watching a drunk person trying to explain the meaning of the universe (and don't it suck that the drunk people always have that nailed but can't clearly explain it to the sober people). So I don't begrudge her the giggling. She understood fast enough that something was very wrong. And she was able to get me help. To get us help. To do my job, essentially.

My children always impressed me. Not in that 'aren't they perfect way' that social media dictates. I don't tend to think I'm an awesome mom, or even a good one on most days. When they were born, my early thoughts were along the lines of "look at you, you perfect being please, please, please don't let me screw you up too much." And more often than not, at the end of the day I think, "I will be a better parent tomorrow. I will. Because today I really sucked it." Given that they've lived with my husband and I for several years now, they are essentially ruined and we are living with our parenting mistakes. Until they turn 18, when I feel comfortable blaming them. After all, I can't take responsibility for you your entire life. "Put a sandwich under your arm and go to work" is a disgusting phrase my grandfather used in lieu of 'grow-up.'

But there is something incredible and unsettling about knowing that your child saved your life. Kind of puts the whole "I carried you for nine months so you better be nice" argument in a different light. When I look at her now, I see someone who is simultaneously so fragile and so strong, it's hard to reconcile them both in the same person. She is stunning, of course, beautiful to me in a singular way that she can't be to anyone else, because I live beside her as she grows. She is all the things that our children are to us – delightful and kind and infuriating and amazing and breathtaking and cute. I believe Mother Nature designed children with the cute built in to help them survive childhood. As in, "if you do that one more time I'm going to kill you." And there is something nearly divine about them when they sleep. A genuine peace, a softness to their features. That can't be a mistake. One look at my sleeping children, and my heart breaks. Aren't they perfect?

So initial giggle notwithstanding, she made the 911 call happen, repeated what the dispatchers weren't getting, clarified, followed instructions, made it all work. In second grade. Without a bit of panic, not a tear to be seen. The result was a lot of unwanted attention at school. An announcement over the loudspeaker, about how proud the principal was, the stares, the questions. Horrified to be asked questions, she sensed, I think, the difference between genuine interest and what is simply an interesting topic of conversation.

> "Oh, your moms in the hospital, huh? Is she really sick?
> Is she going to die? What's wrong with her?"

And she is adamant that it was just a phone call. That she's not heroic. She can't appreciate the scope of being calm under pressure and I hope she never again gets the chance. It wasn't a super easy time for her. Everything was not immediately OK. But she rolled, and asked only one question after each doctor's appointment.

> "Did they fix your heart?"
> "Not yet. Soon."

Until the fun started. I'd say she gave it two, three weeks tops before she started gas-lighting me. That's right. Little bugger started screwing with my head. Like, I'd ask her to go brush her teeth, and she'd walk up to me, dead serious, quizzical look on her face.

> "Mom, what's banana freeze?"
> "Excuse me?"
> "What's banana freeze?"
> "What are you talking about?"
> "You just said banana freeze."
> "No I didn't."
> "Yes, you did. You said, time to— ba-nay-nay freeze."
> "I did not. I definitely did not."
> "You did. Ba-nay. Nay-frizzle. What is that?"
> "That's not what I said".
> "Are you sure you're not having another stroke?"
> "What?"
> "Seriously mom, you could be having another stroke.
> You don't know what you're saying."

Are you kidding me with this? Now I have to worry about my second grader messing with my head. Not cool. By maybe a month after that morning, she simply referred to me as Stroke Woman. Any time I made a mistake. Any time I forgot my keys. Any time my glasses disappeared. Any time at all. Stroke Woman. Way to take the piss out of somebody. Can't wait to hear what she calls me when I'm really old. Of course, I won't be able to hear her. Because I'll turn my hearing aids off. Stroke Woman. That's OK. Next time she asks if they fixed me, I'll tell her "banana frizzle."

It's About Time

I hate being late. Hate it. It makes me extremely uncomfortable. It's deeply rooted in something I will never get to the bottom of because I cannot make appointments with a therapist because the thought of having to be on time for all those appointments is nauseating. And obviously I'm the picture of mental health so why would I need a therapist? What are you implying?

Asked in a theater class to bring in my most hated object, I dug out a wrist watch. For those of you born after 1995, a "wrist watch" is a device you strap onto your wrist in order to tell the time. It does not take calls, make calls, take pictures, make videos, lock your door when you forget, or play your music. Nor does it tell you where you parked your car and how to get home. If you spent a little money on it you could take it in the shower for like ten seconds before remembering and ripping it off your wrist so it didn't get destroyed – that being the "water resistant" model. If you spent a lot of money on it, you could get a water "proof" version and take it down into the depths of the ocean. But only to twenty feet.

Keeping track of time. Bane of my existence. By some miracle, this anxiety did not translate to my biological clock ticking. I hit the snooze on that and kept right on sleeping. Still, the major stress of each evening is considering how many things I need to be on time for the next day. It's the producer in me – this has to happen because this has to happen because this has to happen so the show can go on. On time. 8 p.m., curtain up, no exceptions, no excuses. Curtain up at 8 p.m., even when the asshole I mean actor playing a minor role quits right before final dress rehearsal. 8 p.m., curtain up.

So you can imagine my excitement when I have to arrive for heart surgery on time. What time? Oh, the hospital will call. But when?

When will they call? Oh, the day before. But what time on the day before? The day before.

Great. That. Is. Great. I have no anxiety about that. They'll call the day before. They'll call the day before; they'll let me know. They'll call. They will. They'll call. OK. OK. Not a problem. Don't forget, they'll call. I just have to wait for the call. Where's my phone? "I don't know, Stroke Woman." Remember when phones were plugged into the wall and couldn't run out of batteries? Forget it. I'm not explaining that one. I missed the call. Here's a design flaw for someone to fix – my phone is dead, out of batteries "somewhere" – and I can't call it to find it and plug it in. Lovely Hubby calls me – once the phone was found by my daughter and charged:

> "Hey hon, the hospital called me with our information for tomorrow, but they want you to call them."
> "Call who?"
> "The hospital."
> "But who? Who called?"
> "Here's the number."
> "Who am I asking for?"
> "It's fine, just call. That's what they said-"
> "Oh. K."

A thin layer of sweat covered my entire body.

> "Hi, this is Kimberly, I have surgery tomorrow."
> "Yes, we'll call you."
> "Yes, I know, I'm calling-
> "We will call you regarding your surgery."
> "I understand, but what I have to-"
> "The call nurse has forty-five patients to call regarding surgery. She will call you. You will get a call like everyone else."

In other words, stop tying up the line you absurdly frantic person who thinks that your surgery matters more than anyone else's, just because it's occurring to your body. No one has ever had any anxiety about a surgery, so what's your problem? I lowered my voice, trying to make this curious adversary an accomplice.

> "Right, I understand, the thing is-"

"Ma'am, please allow her to call you."

I spoke faster, certain phone was nearing the cradle, the disconnect imminent.

> "She-did!-She-did.-She-did call.-She-did-call-me-and-she-said-to-call-her-back."
> "You will get a—what?"
> "I was told in the message to call her back."
> "Ah, please hold."

My reward for successfully befriending the phone guard was a list of typical night before surgery instructions: no eating no drinking no wandering the streets arrive four hours ahead of time to wait for six hours to wait to check in. Go to waiting room C for outpatient procedures. Don't go to waiting room B for in-patients and make sure you are in the east wing not the west wing, because the west wing surgeries wait in the A section and if you try to check in there they won't find your records and they will send you home, so make sure you're in the right wing otherwise you could lose a lot of time. And you need to be on time. Oh and Dr. Hockey has offices in both buildings, so if you ask for him they might send you to the wrong place even though he typically doesn't have office hours on the same day as surgery.

Oh dear god. I believe what's left of my brain just exploded. Hopefully the other forty-four patients she had to call today knew what the hell she was talking about.

My parents are in town to hang out with the children and remind me that surgery is serious, and we remembered, responsibly, to mention the surgery to my daughter's teacher so she had a heads up regarding this hospital visit. My daughter went to school, best to be distracted. I pictured her smile when I finally reply to "Did they fix your heart?" with "Yes." I had just enough time to send her off to school and we started to the hospital. Off we go.

Unfortunately, I decided to rely on memory, as did my husband, and we didn't actually go to the right hospital. A bad sense of direction is unbiased in its sabotage and unkind in its timing. We didn't get all the way to the wrong hospital, but we definitely went off course. It's not quite as dumb as it sounds; given how many hospitals and medical facilities we visited (is my likely excuse). At any rate, well done us. When we eventually arrived at the hospital after a car ride that was in no way stressful or filled with accusatory language, there were multiple entrance options. Of course. We avoided the Emergency Room at least, and headed over to the main hospital.

The guard was super helpful. "Dr. Hockey? What a great doc. You know he's a pediatric cardiologist." We did know that, and assured him of that fact as he eyed the back seat, looking for a kid. Still confused by our lack of a little one, he directed, "Dr. Hockey, he's in the other building." Perfect. Off we go.

We drive around to the other building and the equally helpful guard on that side. "Dr. Hockey? He's great. But you know he's pediatrics. He's a pediatric cardiologist. He works with kids. Great doctor. You're not a kid." We parked despite this fact. Off we go.

As we arrived in his office, (my heart was racing at this point) we immediately realized of course we were in the wrong place because he certainly didn't perform heart surgery in his office, he did it in a freaking surgical wing so off we go to back Guard #1 who is shocked that A) we needed to see Dr. Hockey because apparently he works with kids (!!!); B) that I am, in point of fact, there for surgery. Yes, actual surgery. No, not an appointment. And C) we were quite certain this was the entrance we need whether or not we were accompanying minors. Off. We. Go.

I took long deep breaths and desperately tried to avoid checking the time. Not looking, not looking, off we go, not looking. The car was finally parked! In the right lot! At the right hospital! On the right day! -Oh shit! Just kidding. Off we go.

We headed in to find Waiting Room B in the east wing. At check-in, after reassuring us that Dr. Hockey was great we found that - Nope, I'm not on their list. Off we go - they sent us to Waiting Room C, down two floors across the atrium hard right don't go into the cafeteria, where they are also big fans of Dr. Hockey and—I am not on their list either. Here's what I wanted: people who were a little less enamored and a little more helpful. I waited eight weeks to have this frigging thing fixed; it is getting fixed today. They sent us back to the fan club in Waiting Room B, so we went back through the Atrium over the bridge to grandmother's house where we have the option of taking the first open passenger flight in orbit around the moon or board a fucking cruise ship to take us around Cape Horn back through the Panama Canal up the east coast so we can tour the Statue of Liberty. Somewhere in there, I stepped out of the flow of traffic heading back to the elevators and had a minor meltdown. Not woman in the final stages of labor meltdown but a meltdown none-the-less.

> "What is the fucking problem here? Why can't we find the right place?"

To which Lovely Hubby replies:

> "Well, I thought you knew where you were going."
> "I—That you I—WHAT?"
> "I thought you knew where you were going, you spoke to the nurse yesterday. She walked me through everything, and I took notes, but I left them at home because you talked to her."

It is a testament to my upbringing that I did not kill him then and there. *I* spoke to her. That's what we based this treasure hunt on. My recollection of a conversation with a nurse that didn't want to talk to me and thought that I was covered because she had already spoken to the person who was going to take care of me before and after surgery on the day before said surgery. In his defense, I was usually the better of the two of us at finding places.

I disengaged completely at that point. Just get me there. When we returned from safari, I twitched as we arrived in, oh, I don't know, Waiting Room LMNOP. In the right place, and just in time to wait our allotted 900 hours. I slumped, finally there.

"Kimberly?" She called from an office within the office, or more precisely, a corner of the room with three-quarter height walls. She disappeared into it before I got a good look at her. When I entered her five foot by four foot domain, I was in the presence of several things that defied the laws of physics – namely, the size of her lace cuffs, and the number of filing cabinets jammed into the space. It was like seeing Stevie Nicks work at a branch of the Bailey Savings and Loan inside of a phone booth.

It's just Lovely Hubby, myself, Stevie, the computer, the filing cabinets and several thousand plants, which were in turn outnumbered only by the coffee cups littering the desk. It's 9:45 a.m. and Stevie's been here since 1972. Our interview commenced- glamorous, sophisticated, a veritable storm of witty repartee, and completely one-sided. Given the range and detail of queries, I can only conclude that several history and celebrity channels simultaneously planned bio-pics. There's an issue with the computer taking all my data (I'm too much to handle) which she rectified by making huge sweeping motions with the lace cuffs, hooking them on pencils, cups and other table top debris. I realized the mouse wasn't quite reaching the surface of the desk. It hovered, unwilling to make contact. Hmm… I may know what's wrong with the computer… She hasn't looked at me once. I could be a zebra for all Stevie Cuffs knows. We review pages and pages of disclaimers, warnings, and sonnets written to enlighten and terrify me: 'You can't say we didn't warn you! Medical things are happening here and you are agreeing to them – ANYTHING can go wrong. Here for a heart procedure? You might leave with a baby. Don't say we didn't warn you.' What a mind fuck. Oh, and we'll give you a pile of linguistic spaghetti worthy of congress right before your super important life saving procedure to sign, since you're clearly in a great state of mind to be making this decision.

Ever wondered why they don't give you that paperwork ahead of time? So you could actually consider it carefully? In essence, surgery is a two-step process:

1) Doctor informs patient that they need a procedure and patient agrees.
2) Legal spends the intervening time prior to the procedure telling patient not to do it, because this shit is dangerous. This is a hospital. People die here.

We escape Stevie Cuffs before the encore and head back to the waiting room where we—"Kimberly?" And I'm up. Maybe there's merit in being late. No waiting. My college roommate may have been onto something. Gowns and machines and giving blood oh my! Lots of nurses, none of note until Natasha.

Ah, Natasha. She arrived with a blood pressure cuff and a thick Russian accent (is there any other kind?). While one nurse worked my vitals on a large machine to my left and periodically updated her online status, Natasha ran me through her version of get to know the patient. Oh, and the accent? Make it thick. Boris & Natasha thick.

> "OK, how are you today? Good? Good. I'll take your blood pressure, OK? Good? Good. All right, now, just a few more of these."

She applied my favorite heart octopus monitoring pads. Sticky sticky sticky. Finished with her art project we moved on to small talk.

> "OK, you're good, everything is good? Family is good?"

It's nice of her to ask, given she's never met them.

> "Who is here today?"

Ah, that's why.

> "Your husband? Good. Good. You have a brother? I have a brother. Oh, I love him but we fight fight fight. When we were kids. So much fighting. You fight. No? Come on, yes, of course. Of course you fight, brother and sister fight. And not – um – argue, we fight. Fight. Oh, yes. We broke all the furniture. All the furniture in the house, broken. We fighting and the chair is broken and the table is broken and my mother she is crying and yelling and yelling and crying so much everything is broken. She says, 'no no no, my children, oh, my children, they hate each other, oh no no no.' No, no, we don't hate. Hey, we love each other. We love each other, and we fight. We fight, and break furniture, because love each other."

Because they love each other? She chose this moment to whip out an electric razor and lift the blanket.

> "OK, I shave you now."

I reply, "I'm sorry." Honestly, I don't know what I was supposed to say? Yippee? Thank you? Can you do my initials? It's a necessary process for a procedure that starts in the groin, patients cannot, after all, resemble gorillas. In all seriousness, there's nothing funny or descriptive to say about grooming female pubic hair that wasn't said perfectly in Steve Martin's *Shop Girl.* This author, and everyone else, need not bother.

After the extended-play pre-surgery version of 'please identify yourself' they wheeled me to wait in a hallway. Dr. Hockey stops by to chat. He looked beat. Uh oh. It was a tough morning with a very young patient. He had three patients today, but there won't be a hat trick. I decided to be the easy patient. He met with me, reviewed the process – closed his eyes while he described what he has to do. I assumed he's visualizing the procedure. Or perhaps I was too stunning that morning in my hospital gown. The geometric design made me look like the cover of an algebra book. Or maybe my dreadlock returned and he's afraid of it. Tough to tell. I didn't interrupt his concentration. He can close his eyes while we talk, he can stand on one leg and squawk like a chicken. As long as he gets the job done.

In the operating room, snuggled under a warm blanket, I became invisible. I don't know if it's because they sedate the younger patients before they arrive or what, but the staff acted like I was already unconscious. One of the nurses was a runner, and she had a lot to say about herself. Is she trying to impress Dr. Hockey? Get it all in before I get there sister. I'm the only groin he's going to be interested in once I arrive. Here's what I learned about her in the tiny amount of time I was nearby and/or in the room: first, she runs marathons. Second, she likes a glass or two of wine at night, and does the good doctor also enjoy wine? 'Never the night before a procedure' (thank you!). Third, she didn't run this last marathon but if she had run it, she would have won. This last is to another nurse while they press buttons, move tubes and generally monkey around the table, and I lay there thinking, hey, could you pretend to concentrate on me? I gathered by her marathon comments that she runs, she runs fast, and she runs for very long distances. Despite this I knew she wouldn't last long in a Zombie Apocalypse. The entirely self-involved never do. Speaking of self-involved, her bragging made me think of my scenario, like, oh yeah, you might have won that marathon, unless you have a PFO that decided to fall apart at that exact moment. Then you're just like me. Except for the fact that you can run a marathon. And you have, you know, medical skills. OK, fine, her athletic ability was impressive and I was jealous. Could we just stop talking about her? I need to concentrate on my procedure.

The anesthesiologist was not in the room yet. We waited, some with more patience than others. I snuggled under the warm blanket, but Dr. Hockey paced increasingly faster circles. I found it very comforting. It reminded me of when I was an athlete. Everyone has a pre-game ritual. Dr. Simple eventually arrived (my anesthesiologist). Quite nice, and I can tell he speaks to a lot of children because his description of the procedure is super simplified? OK? I'm going to have a couple of tubes down my throat? One for breathing? And one to see what's going on? (intubate and a trans esophageal echo- got it). But I don't have to worry about that; all I have to do is have a short nap, OK? Ah, the napping. The best part. See you on the other…

People really do cough hard when they pull that tube out, that's not just TV. Nurse Marathon said it was a piece of cake, less than ten minutes for the entire procedure. She seemed mildly impressed, with me or Dr. Hockey I'm not sure, but I was pleased to be in the boring section of the medical manual. I'd had too many weeks of not fitting into an easy category.

I was, in fact, a brilliant patient. My arteries were accommodating, my heart willing, even the PFO itself perfectly situated and simply fixed. The procedure to fix something broken for 44+ years clocked in at around ten minutes. "On camera" for less than two minutes, meaning they positioned the device that fast. One minute and forty-six seconds to be exact. Easy peasy. Dr. Hockey earned a hug from Lovely Hubby for his efforts. And I'm sure, you know, there was some kind of remuneration involved here somewhere.

All that's left today is for me to prove I'm perfect by taking a few laps around the ICU, and of course, the requisite pee. Everybody loves a working pair of kidneys. I crush the ICU lap record in a blistering three minutes fifty-two seconds. And I totally know how to pee.

Delighted, we were approached by only one nurse for our exit interview, and she was mercifully brief. If you're going to turn over heart surgery patients in less than a day, ya gotta be quick. We hit a teeny hiccup when she mentions my "ASD."

> "Excuse me? My what?"
> "The ASD repair you had today." Hubby and I shared a look. We don't know what that is. Literally have never heard the term ASD. Not once in these past eight weeks. Huh.
> "Well, no, as a matter of fact. I don't know what that is. I had a PFO repair."

She gets a disconcertingly concerned look on her face.

"I'll be right back."

Oh my god. Hubby and I entertain the possibility that my surgery was so quick because it wasn't the right one? Pause while we share a laugh over that insane possibility.

No, all is well. She returns to clarify that ASD (Atrial Septal Defect) is the grown-up term, more or less, for PFO (Patent Foramen Ovale). Outstanding. I had the right surgery, we gave this poor young nurse a near heart attack, and I have a new acronym. Woo hoo! Time to go home.

Spare Parts, or Zombie Leftovers

I left the hospital with a Band-Aid on my leg. An actual, honest to goodness Band-Aid. Nothing special, nothing that screamed 'heart surgery' or even 'surgery' or anything remotely life threatening. I had more bandages when my wisdom teeth were removed. I left with what you give your kid when they have an ow-ee. What's the matter honey? Oh, you broke your brain? OK, OK, I'll get you something for your boo boo. It's disconcerting, and frankly anti-climactic. And for that, I'm grateful. It did make for odd conversation when people saw me walking around the next day. I felt compelled to justify being upright; after all, heart surgery sounds like something that should keep you down for at least a day or so. I suspected that they suspected that I was just in it for the free dinners that so many nice people brought us. Note – if you are ever part of a meal train – hands down best dinner we received was cooked taco meat and all the fixings. Like an island, rising from a delightful sea of baked pasta.

I wouldn't trade my Band-Aid for something dire of course, but it does make me wonder, invisible as it is, what did I lose? I got the better end of the deal, whatever it was. But it begs the question. It reminds me of an old game where you ask a friend, what would you trade for a million dollars? Would you trade a body part? What if you didn't get to pick which one? Would you trade a pinkie? A thumb? An earlobe? An organ?

I've wondered what was taken from me that morning. For a time, I lost my sense of security in my own body. That didn't last long, thankfully. But it's a strange, strange feeling. Particularly for someone who still thinks like an athlete, despite current evidence. I couldn't entirely trust my body. Right now, you probably assume you can walk, if you are over eighteen months of age (and if you are a toddler reading this, good for you!) Walking is just something that we do. And speaking. You likewise think that if you open your mouth to speak, the words you expect to hear will come out. I think it, I say it. Or more often, I say it and then I think about it. Either way, there is a connection between brain and mouth. So when neither of those things function for a while, in spite of your brains best effort, it gives you an appreciation of the mechanics of it all. I knew exactly what I was trying to say and it just wasn't happening. Yet every other day of my 44+ years, no problem. A remarkably well-designed machine. And my machine was back in working order very quickly for all intents. A few minutes for my speech to return, a few hours for my legs to be entirely trustworthy. Many more nights wondering about my heart, but again, fixable. I felt whole. Entire. An entity.

So what did I lose? What did I lose. I'll never know precisely of course. I know that one of the clots was in my speech center. It wasn't slurred, my brain invented a language on the spot. Yet I can still say I love you, and that's all that really matters if you really think about it- hold on, I just threw up in my mouth a little bit. It doesn't seem to be in a part of my brain that holds long-term memory. I can still remember absurdly far back into my childhood, I can still remember entire conversations.

However, I can no longer make a mental note, though this may simply be age, or peri-menopause, or one of 9,000 absurd distinctions that designate getting older. Mental notes are no longer possible for me. And that word on the tip of your tongue? I never get it. It never comes. I leave a lot of blanks and "TBAs" in my writing. Placeholders for finding the right whatchamacallit. So now I explain, define, dance around it, toss out possibilities, try to make it pop out of my head. And it still won't come. So you have to make do with a word that's not the right word, it's not wrong, but it's just not exactly right. It's the next-door neighbor of the word I want. Which would be an issue, if I were a writer or something. Really dodged a projectile of ammunition there.

What if you lost something, and you didn't know what it was? Would you miss it? Would it bug you not to know? You see the problem? I'd like to say that my stroke took away my temper. Or my lack of organization. Or my tendency to make piles of papers/objects/clothes to be dealt with 'later'. But no such luck. I have been waiting to discover what it is, exactly, that died that morning.

It may have been the last shreds of my patience. I've never had an exceptionally patient attitude with customer service. Five cross-country moves puts me on the phone with these folks a lot. A lot. But I am now reaching dragon lady levels of volume and exasperation. And I've been, frankly, hurtful. "Listen. I understand that you have absolutely no power and you must follow the script in front of you, leaving you no real ability to handle, well, anything or solve anyone's issue in any sense of the word, so please, do us both a favor and get your manager on the phone. I know you'd like to help me, or you've been programmed to pretend you'd like to help me, but we both know you don't. You CAN'T. YOU CANNOT HELP ME GET YOUR MANAGER. I have concerns about your ability to hear and comprehend – you can't help me. YOU CAN'T HELP ME. GET SOMEONE TO SOLVE THIS. No problem, I'll hold." It doesn't work by the way. Honey still catches more flies.

Perhaps I lost my needless worry about the little things – it definitely had an impact. In a cherish every moment kind of way, I was a great mom for about a week after returning home from the hospital. Totally patient. Yes, my youngest child, I can wait over here with your pants and your shoes while you adjust an infinite number of blocks into just the right configuration. And I'll do it with a smile on my face. Just complete gratitude for being there, and who cares if we're late for everything because no one puts anything where it goes and I'm the only one that ever plans a meal or keeps track of our social calendar or knows where anything is oh my god, nothing better ever happen to me or the sky will fall down. My abundant gratitude and the calm that comes with it lasted a week. Maybe. And I was right back to "making it all happen."

But the sky didn't fall down. And while my heart shatters to think of my children without me, the fact is that my daughter got to school without me getting her there. For several days. With lunch. And clothing. And she even made it to the science fair. And my son's diapers were changed. He was also fed, clothed and napped appropriately. Eating, sleeping, playing, homework. It all happened with no input whatsoever.

Am I pretending that I'm expendable? No. Not entirely – I know my children are better off for having me here and I know that my partner and I are better for sharing our journey. But I am saying that no matter how integral you are to the lives around you, don't forget that you're still just damn lucky to be there. And god forbid something did happen to you, yes, it would be crushing. But guess what, eventually, *they would get over it.* Not in the sense that they would forget you – I'm sure someday there will be a few statues erected for me, perhaps a memorial marathon run by sobbing thousands. Or more likely, a memorial saunter from the couch to the fridge. But truly- don't you want your tribe to be able to move forward? Could there be anything worse than to think of your loved ones trapped in the moment you left, forever frozen in grief? I'm not saying a few general sniffles wouldn't be nice, but the full on snot running down your face sobbing should be as brief as possible. Like, momentary. Snot is gross.

So what did I lose that day? What died? I suspect I'm going to find out one day, like forgetting about a houseplant only to abruptly discover its brittle, collapsing remains.

What would I choose to lose? Ah. My temper, my ass (I'm being honest. This isn't about what culture tells me I should look like, it's about what annoys me when I'm getting dressed and my shit doesn't fit, and frankly I'm too busy to buy new shit), my general bitchiness, my ability to hold on to whatever is currently annoying me about my husband, my slight tendency toward drama, my even slighter tendency toward hyperbole. No, I actually enjoy that last bit of myself.

I may have lost my ability to hold my tongue around strangers. It was a fragile hold to begin with. I am far more reactive to situations, angrier at the little injustices of life and simultaneously grateful to be here. I'm sickened by the human capacity for cruelty.

I wouldn't mind losing my total lack of self-discipline. Deadlines for others? No problem. Deadlines for me? Not so much.

None of this really matters, in the grand scheme, because I'm fine. Physically I'm fine. And mentally I'm fine. Mostly. I'm fine.

What died that day? They told me the spot on my brain that died was tiny. That was the actual word used "tiny." I never asked how tiny is tiny. Or the real question, how big is tiny? Is tiny a pinhead? Is tiny the size of a dime? A nickel? And why is a nickel bigger than a dime, is there anything more confusing? And does the size of it matter? Since we don't know exactly which part of our brain makes us who we are, are there pieces that are… expendable? If there are, I'd like to know. May as well be able to offer the zombies an appetizer instead of an entrée, right?

What would you give up, your ability to speak, your ability to hear, or your ability to see? Someday it won't matter, because we'll be able to regenerate matter. Brain matter that is. And of course, we won't ask if we should, we will do it because we can. Or the flip side of this question, what would it kill you to lose? If you lost memories, would you be content with photographs? We are told to let go of the past, but the past is what shapes us, it's our frame of reference. If you don't know how you got there, is it possible to know where you are? Your ability to form relationships? Who are you, if not part of a larger web of humans, if you aren't connecting with humans? I crave solitude. I always have. And sometimes I feel downright anti-social. That's hasn't changed. But my willingness to suppress that side of myself and force myself to be social has changed. I extend more invitations. Life's a little brighter; the laundry detergent smells a little better – blah blah blah.

I never had patience for willful ignorance. For deliberate, stick your head in the sand stupidity. I never had patience with people who don't use their gifts, and yet my own ability to procrastinate is Olympian. Were there an actual competition, I would have won gold if I had finished filling out my application, like I planned to, only I never got to the store that day to get pens, because I ignored that little blinking warning light on my car. For eight months.

So what did I lose that day?

Perhaps the thing that died that day was the last bit of hope of my own invincibility. That childhood dream that I'd be the one to outwit decay. Maybe. Maybe I still will. After all, I survived the MRI and I have two fail proof ways to outwit zombies. Outwitting the brain dead. Takes one to know one.

Other Brain Dead Times, or Leftover Zombie Leftovers

Before we leave, I must divulge that this was not my only brain dead moment. It was my first (and second and third) neurological event, but alas, I've spent many a moment without a brain. Full disclosure, I adore the Scarecrow from *The Wizard of Oz*. He walks, he talks, he sings, he makes friends, and get this – no brain. I used to sing "If I Only Had a Brain" with great gusto and made-up lyrics I won't punish you with here. Perhaps I've always known I'd be a little brain dead. I am not a moron, mind you, I know when to stop the lather, rinse, repeat cycle and the instructions on hair dryers (do not operate in a drawer) and chainsaws (do not stop with genitals) are not written for me. You don't have to tell me my coffee's hot! It isn't hot, though, because I put it down on the back steps when I went to feed the dog and now I don't know where it is.

I won't pretend that I've got it all together, or that I even remember where it is. Let's ease into my non-stroke idiocy slowly:

I give the dog food to the cat and vice versa. Not horrible. Except that the dog is extremely allergic to everything except her food. Eh. Details.

I occasionally look for my glasses as they sit perched on my head. It happens.

I put the cereal in the refrigerator and the milk in the cupboard. But not for long, I fix it before the milk spoils.

I've been known to stand in a room, completely flabbergasted as to why I walked in there in the first place, leave the room, remember what I needed, walk back in, and stand there in bewilderment. But I was pregnant (and baby brain is real but that's a different book).

I have, on occasion, been unable to introduce family members to friends because I can't remember either of their names. Long term family members, like say, siblings and long term friends, like say, the godparents of my children.

I once spent ten minutes looking for my phone while on the phone with my sister. Likewise, I tried to make a call on a calculator. Yeah, I 'dialed' the number on the calculator on my phone, but still, why wouldn't they pick up?

I've been known to leave the car door open. More than once. And more than one door. Just now, Lovely Hubby walked in with my wallet. "Missing this?" Huh. Where was it? "Lying in the middle of the driveway." Hmmm…

My imagination is occasionally over-active. The time my necklace unhooked and I may have freaked out slightly because, for some bizarre reason, it felt like a snake was sliding around under my shirt. While I was driving. How I thought that a snake got into my car and up my shirt while I was driving 40 miles an hour is for the professionals to figure out.

Mind you, all of this is pre-stroke. I'm going to stop now before someone sends medical help for me and protective services for my children. Let's look a little further; she then contradicted herself, underscoring her lack of a brain.

Imagine a woman, who looks something like me, alone in a New York hotel room. If you don't know what I look like, just know that she looks Amazing. She's in town to work on a show, enjoying a few days of the rare solitude that only a long married person who is also a parent can truly savor.

Her room is an ordinary size, which for New York means none of the doors open fully because they slam into furniture– and one is required to stand on the bed to open the drawer, stand on the nightstand to open the door, and so forth. But the bathroom – the bathroom, by some miracle, is huge. A completely strange shape, of course, this odd pointy triangle with a section of real estate at the end that accommodates nothing, but it's heavy on the square footage nonetheless.

She's going through her morning ritual, dancing a little, singing a little, who can see? Who can hear? Who can care? Gargling is the most fun, how many different sounds can she make? In a fit of exuberance, she throws her head back gargling open mouthed, losing a little slime out the corner of her mouth but whatever, she's alone.

Laughing. Her husband would enjoy witnessing this. Perhaps she will perform a mouthwash concert for him when she returns home. Hmm… I'm sure there's a dirty gargling joke in there somewhere, but no matter. She throws her head forward full speed to spit and SLAMS her forehead on the faucet. Slams it hard. Skull meets faucet at 183 mph. Slumping to the floor, she realizes she is not unconscious, but rather painfully aware of the mint green foam now running down the front of her only clean shirt. Stunned, frothing, she imagines being found in a few hours, days perhaps, with no company meantime but the sound of her own ridicule. If I wasn't in so much pain, I'd have peed myself laughing, ruining my only clean pair of pants.

But that's not the brain dead part. The brain dead part is that I've just told you this story. No one ever had to know. In truth, it was a moment of silliness, a miscalculation in the distance from forehead to faucet. It could happen to anyone. It might happen to anyone. Just a mistake, really. Like a friend working on the set of a play who screwed himself to the ceiling. That's right, I said ceiling. And he was stuck there, all alone, hand pinned between board and ceiling, stretched out from the ladder. You know you've done it. But he told me. And I told you. Keeping your stupidity to yourself may be an excellent indicator of mental health, which is why politicians and most of the media should not be allowed to speak. What makes it truly brain dead is the sharing of this personal stupidity.

So let's continue! Another of my top brain dead moments was my hospitalization. For dehydration. For those of you unaware of this rare disease, dehydration is caused by a lack of "water." I know, it's shocking, but not as shocking as what comes next. To prevent this debilitating nightmare from descending upon you, you must drink "water."

I'll give you a moment.

It's not as easy as it sounds. You have to find a source of water, and really, who has running water readily available here in the pre-Zombie Apocalyptic United States in the 21st century? It's unheard of. It's mythical – ooh, travel through the living room to the kitchen… go to the cupboard… get a glass. Search and search for a faucet, where could it be? All the while fighting zombies and centaurs and dragons and various politicians for the right to water. Come on! It's not easy. OK, if you live in California, as I now do, fighting for water is no laughing matter. But my dehydration was pre-drought and therefore self-induced.

OK, here's what actually happened. I got sick. Caught a cold. Lovely Hubby was working nights, so I was lolling around with a low fever for weeks. Just could not kick my cold. And I tried all the usual stuff, like OTC remedies. Then, I started with the homeopathic remedies. Then, I started getting desperate. I know, I know. I'll SWEAT it out of me – and off I went To Exercise. Did it work? Not so much, no. Those weeks are a blur, I was going to work, I was coming home and falling into bed, there was an attempt to eat food occasionally, and just kick this damn thing.

When Lovely Hubby and I were finally home at the same time, we had a little chat, "I still don't feel well." "Yeah, you don't look well. Why don't you have a glass of wine, take a shower, and I'll call the doctor." Why not? We're Italian. Doesn't a little red wine cure everything? Spoiler: It does not cure dehydration. Not at all.

I took a shower. Exhausting, this shower was (and it turned me into Yoda). Absolutely wiped out I am – the soap, the washing of the hair. An endless cycle of lather, rinse, repeat. So tired, so very tired, must keep rinsing... I stepped out to dry off and bam – I had to vomit, right there, right then. So I leaned back over the bathtub.

Let me explain – we lived in a charming apartment with a split bathroom – shower and sink in one tiny room, commode in another tiny room. So there I am, a room away from the toilet, holding onto the shower curtain to prevent landing in my own vomit when it arrives. Why is waiting to throw up so much worse than throwing up? So much worse. I would rather throw up five times than wait to throw up once. Lovely Hubby enters, still holding the phone.

"Um. Are you OK?"
"No, I think I'm going to puke."
"In the bathtub?"
"Yes."
"Why not use the toilet?"
"I can't get to the toilet, I'm too tired."
"OK. Hold on… the doctor says we should go to the Emergency Room."
"Huh. OK. I think I need clothes."

Ah the joy of being with someone who truly loves and cares for you – they can watch you try to vomit in a bathtub and then pick out some unders for you, so you don't have to go butt ass naked into the Emergency Room. Clothes are put on my body as I lie face-planted on the bed and we head to the car, parked some distance away, after all this is San Francisco and a street cleaning day. I exited our apartment with no problem, very proud of myself, up two steps, through the garden, down two steps, I thought I was doing really well but apparently I was wobbling just a tiny bit so Lovely Hubby helped me along. Like the kind of help where you put an arm around someone and take all of their body weight, and the totally fine person just has to shuffle their feet. Like a drunk person.

"Wait, wait, wait. I just need to lie down here for a minute."

'Here' being the hood of a random car.

"What, ah… what are you doing hon?"
"Just for a second. I just need a minute – oh, it's nice and cool. Give me a second."

I quietly rested my cheek on the car hood, and half of my body. Ahhhhhh. Nice and cool.

"I think we should go to the hospital."
"I just need a little rest."

After my nap we got into the car and over to the hospital. It's a Saturday night – a Saturday night in an Emergency Room in a Big City. The droopy tired girl with the nice husband is not a priority. As we wait, I have an overwhelming desire to lie down, and proceed to do so. On the floor. Of the waiting room. Which, as you know, is super sanitary, prompting the popular phrase – 'so clean it was like the floor of an ER waiting room' or some such thing. We wait for all the gunshot victims, and heart attack victims, and childbirth victims, and the idiot who fell off a ladder (more on him elsewhere). My husband, who is no longer Lovely but now Really Grouchy Husband, insists that I sit in a chair rather than lying on the floor. Apparently I am embarrassing him from down here on the floor. So touchy! Good grief. Fine, FINE! I'll sit in a chair. But I'm going to slump way, way, way down. Waaaaay down. So my ass is hanging off, my torso is on the seat of the chair, and just my head is sticking up. There. That feels better.

I finally got admitted and we found out – shocker – that I'm dehydrated. The level of fluid in my veins is so low that my body is literally demanding that I make things easier on my heart – hence my overwhelming desire to get my body horizontal. My blood pressure is taken while lying down, and then standing up. The nurse doesn't even finish the standing blood pressure before she's telling me to lie down. Apparently she doesn't want me passing out on her. And in case you're wondering, you can't just drink a glass of water to fix this, although of course water is the cure. Once you are dehydrated, you need big, big, big amounts of fluid to make up the deficit. Particularly if you are still running a low-grade fever. They start an IV of solution right away, and tell me not to stand up for any reason because they are fairly certain I'll drop on my ass.

"Let me know when you have to pee."

Will do. And that solution bag is done.

"Gotta pee?"
"Nope."

Bag number two, up, on, in, done.

"Gotta pee?"
"Nope."

Bag number three, up, on, in, done.

"Gotta pee?"
"Nope."

And these are big bags, mind you. Not that tiny shit they show on TV. It takes forever for them to drip in. Bag number four, up, on, in, done.

"Seriously, do you have to pee now?"
"Um, yeah, I could use the bathroom."

Success! Pee! You realize that my diagnosis and the subsequent waiting for me to pee is essentially what they do with newborns – infants nurse and the parents anxiously wait to see if junior will pee, signifying that the innards are working. This is monitored for infants. Helpless little monkeys a few hours old. I am more than a few hours old. The cure for my disease is called water. Available, attainable, accessible.

Fine. I accept my stupidity. I'm given my marching papers. Drink a lot of fluids. Rest. Drink more. In fact, stay in bed for two entire days do not get up except to pee. Not seriously? Seriously. Drink everything you can, except caffeine and alcohol, and don't get up except to pee.

So there you have it. I was hospitalized for dehydration. Twice.

The second time – Oh. Did you need a minute? Go ahead, laugh. I'll wait, because I understand. I understand that it takes a moment to contemplate the level of stupid required for this event to happen A SECOND TIME.

Ready?

I would like to take this moment to thank whoever invented the airsickness bag. A bit of context for you – I was working at a start up in Silicon Valley, literally starting it up, and simultaneously running my theater production company on the east coast. I'd fly back and forth, roughly every four or five days. It sounds very glamorous unless you don't actually have 'people' taking care of your 'stuff.' Like eating. And drinking. And sleeping. I was burning the candle at both ends, hell; I was burning the middle and the box it came in. If I were stretched any thinner I'd be cellophane.

I started vomiting on the flight from Boston to St. Louis, where I was supposed to make my connecting flight to LA. I would like to formally apologize to my seatmates – a father and daughter enjoying her first experience on an airplane. Enjoying may be an overstatement. If I could have gotten to the bathroom without passing out I would have. After a blurry flight of cold sweats and warm puke, we landed.

In the terminal, I immediately ask for a First Aid station? A nurse? Any kind of anyone with some medical experience? A cot where I can lie down? No? All righty then. I'll just get on my connecting flight. I am mid-conversation with the flight attendant on the new plane, requesting the seat closest to the bathroom when I am interrupted by a sprint to said bathroom. Thanks anyway, I think I'm going to have to sit this one out.

Back in the terminal. My options are: (A) sit there. (B) Get on a flight. (C) Go to the hospital. Fine. I need the hospital; I'll admit it. My options are (a) take a cab. (b) Take an ambulance. I really don't want to pass out in a cab, that feels like the opening of a crime procedural. So I choose ambulance. Poor choice.

It's not a wheelchair I'm offered. It's a high back chair with multiple seat belts. One for my waist. One for my legs – oh, okay. One for my arms. Really, because I'm not – OK fine. And one for my forehead. What? I said forehead. OK, OK, that's fine. I'm fine. It's not like they're going to wheel me passed all the other passengers waiting to board – oh my god. They're wheeling me passed all the other passengers, down the ramp. Down. The. Ramp.

You think you've been embarrassed? You haven't. Not until you've been strapped into a chair like Hannibal Lecter at his hungriest. Down the ramp. Past the passengers (average passenger jet holds what, 150 people? 250 people?) I'm too tired to try and look dangerous, so I settle for bemused. My eyelids lower to slits so I can peek at my surroundings then – oh good lord – I'm being flipped onto my back down the stairs headfirst - we have to exit onto the tarmac via the door at the end of the ramp – and they are taking me headfirst, on my back, down a flight of very steep stairs - is this some kind of punishment? Or the inspiration for a new rollercoaster?

Our cool sirens screaming us off the tarmac appeased me, and I apologize for all the flight delays that day. That one time in St. Louis when you were stuck? That was me. I would also like to apologize for anyone nice enough to say a prayer for 'that poor soul in the ambulance' as we sped by numerous windows full of waiting passengers. No need, thank you anyway, but no need for your prayers. Just a dumb ass who can't figure out how to drink water.

The Emergency Room doc is unimpressed. Not only was I a boring case, I was a boring self-diagnosing case. He left to flirt with someone as soon as possible. I got to call a cab back to the airport after only two bags of fluid (I'm learning!).

The third time-

Kidding. I'm kidding. Probably.

Leftover Leftover Zombie Leftovers or the Epilogue

Thirty days after my surgery Dr. Hockey pronounced me "seamless." My heart is whole. More importantly, I am cleared for any and all rollercoasters, and those little signs that say 'people with fucked up hearts can't do this'? – those do not apply.

Eight weeks of total mayhem, now return to your normally scheduled life. What was I doing before all this? Ah, yes. Breakfast.

Very Serious Appendix A

Would your child know what to do in an emergency? You have a house fire plan, and an earthquake, tornado, or hurricane plan as needed for your area. You have all the medical info needed for your kid in any situation – school, camp, sports, and activities.

Do you have a plan for when the grown up in the house has a medical emergency and cannot speak? No?

Consider – your child needs:

1) To know how to call 9-1-1, and that does not mean just dialing. Do they know:
   — How to make an emergency call on your cell phone?
   — What information to give? At the least, your address or location, or the ability to read it (see below).
   — That they must stay on the line with 9-1-1?
2) Access to your medical information:
   — An easily accessible, one page document with all the critical information for every member of your family.
   — Printed in advance, updated regularly, and reachable – like on the refrigerator door. When the EMT's arrive, they can hand them the paper. I don't like to display my medical info, so we keep ours on the inside of a lower cabinet, within reach.
3) Your emergency page includes everything you can think of that would help the medical team, including but not limited to – name, date of birth, blood type, allergies, any medical condition, any medications or prescriptions, doctors names, numbers and their hospital affiliations, health insurance.
4) Also include the name and number of every adult living in the house, every person living in

the house, emergency contact name and numbers and the name and number of someone very close by who can come and take care of the kids

5) Practice. Practice. Practice.
    a. Practice actually making a call – use a general situation, like my friend Suzy fell out of a tree and there are no grown ups around.
    b. Practice with your child making the 'call' and you being the dispatcher.
    c. Practice asking the questions the dispatcher will ask – where are you? What happened?
    d. Practice staying on the line with the dispatcher until they tell you to hang up.

My daughter was barely eight years old when she received this training with her troop. A month later she saved my life.

Very Serious Appendix B

A stroke is a serious, life threatening medical event and should not be taken lightly. I was in an ambulance within minutes of my symptoms appearing, and you should be just as quick with your response.

The American Stroke Association (strokeassociation.org) offers updated information on stroke symptoms, diagnostic tools and advances in treatment guidelines. The American Heart Association (heart.org) offers heart health guidelines and information on a variety of heart health related questions. As of this writing, both websites are sharing new guidelines for stroke patient treatments related to clot dissolving medicines and mechanical thrombectomy (the mechanical removal of a clot).

The general guidelines for stroke symptoms use the acronym F.A.S.T.

F.A.S.T.

F – Face Drooping

A – Arm Weakness

S – Speech Difficulty

T – Time to call 911

Update:
The National Stroke Association has added difficulty with B (Balance) and E (Eyes) to their list of stroke symptoms. Information changes often - please visit their website for the latest descriptions and acronyms:

B.E. F.A.S.T.

DISCLAIMERS (read this section first)

I am not a medical expert. I am not even a medical novice. I'm like a medical fetus. If you take anything in this book as medical advice you are a moron. If you are a moron, please do the following:

1) Send me your bank account and bank routing numbers, along with your social security number and any passwords to online financial accounts that you have. Please alphabetize the list of online accounts, if in fact you know the alphabet.
2) Go seek actual medical advice from medical professionals. You may want to start with someone who can tell you why you are stupid enough to take medical advice from a woman who titled her book "I'm a Little Brain Dead."

Further Disclaimers

1. Typose are the result of said condition. Including that one. So don't get picky. You see what I did there?
2. Any mention of real people living (Hugh Laurie) or real people living among the undead (Norman Reedus) are completely intentional yet in no way imply that they endorse this work or me in any way. They are both, after all, highly skilled artists in more than one area and I am just a little brain dead.
3. If you're reading along and there's a reference that you just don't get, don't fret. You're not having a stroke. You just need to catch up on *The Walking Dead* currently airing on AMC (based on the graphic novels by Robert Kirkman and Tony More). Well, you don't have to catch up. I'm not going to force you. It's not like they need your viewership. The apocalypse is doing quite well on its own, thank you very much.
4. Likewise, references to the television show *House* owe themselves to the series produced by David Shore which aired on FOX from 2004-2012.

Acronyms – Acronyms, or ACRNMSs, are a key part of the medical world. They consist of the first letters of either words or pieces of medical terms, and they serve several purposes. First, to maintain an air of medical mystery. Second, to double the work load on med students as they memorize a nickname for everything they just memorized. Third, to halve the work load of actors playing doctors so they don't have to memorize the real terms, which cannot be pronounced without sounding like you have Braca's Aphasia.

Acute CVA – a stroke resulting in damage (i.e., dead) brain tissue. I prefer to think of it as brain cells instead of tissue, because it just sounds like a smaller area. Often confused with TIA. Mine, like most people's, was cryptogenic, as in, we will never be one hundred percent sure why this happened.

ASD – Atrial Septal Defect. For everyone not practicing medicine, the end game on this is similar to a PFO. The septum isn't as much like a wall as it should be. This version is a congenital heart defect, because the septum between the two atria didn't form.

Braca's Aphasia – when you know exactly what you're saying, but no one else does. Because the Braca region of your brain is damaged. See 'incredibly frustrating' for more.

Endoscopic – basically any procedure that uses a skinny tube fed into an organ instead of cutting. In my case, a tube that went in through an artery in my leg and up to my heart.

Factor V Leiden – a genetic mutation that may or may not make your blood hyper coagulate.

Hyper Coagulate – Essentially, sticky blood. Coagulation is the medical term for blood clotting, which is a good thing when you have a cut, but a bad thing for general every day health. Clots jam up the system. There shouldn't be a rush hour in your body.

MRI – Magnetic Resonance Imagery. Yet another way to look inside your body without cutting you open. Keep your eyes closed, and when they ask you if you are claustrophobic, the answer is yes. I'm sure, in a planned situation, this metal tube is an enjoyable experience. Think of it like a tanning bed without the UV rays.

Migration of a Thrombus - There's no acronym for this but I adore the phrase. It refers to the route a clot takes. I can't help but imagine my three clots as a Herd of Thrombi, which may have been the name of Lovely Hubby's first band. HOT is the acronym, which I'm almost certain was the name of their first single.

PFO (Patent Foramen Ovale) – commonly referrered to as a hole in your heart. It may actually be a hole, or it may be a flap that didn't seal, or it may be some version between the two. Many, many people (I heard as low as one out of three but one out of four people seems to be the commonly cited number) have a PFO and live their whole lives none the wiser.

TEE (Trans Esophageal Echocardiogram) – a better look at your heart than an Echocardiogram. Involves a tube down your throat, and if it's a TOE (worst acronym ever) it also involves a contrast material so all the little bits of your heart show up clearly. Your esophagus is nicely positioned to give a great view of your heart, no ribs in the way.

TPAs: Clot busting drugs that have a time limit on when they can be administered. So get your ass, and your brain, to a hospital at the first sign of stroke. As of this writing, those time limits may be changing. Ask an actual medical professional for more information.

TIA: TransIschemic Attack – all the fun of a stroke while it's happening with none of the permanent brain damage. What everyone assumes you mean when you are forty-four and say you had a stroke.

In Gratitude

Thank you IDB for saving my life.

Thank you Renee for teaching her how.

Thank you first responders on Long Island – who are volunteers – for all that you do, and for making sure I didn't fall on my face down the front steps.

Thank you Jenn for dropping everything to help my kids.

Thank you Robert Kirkman for your brain, whose creativity literally helped my brain deal with its own little zombie apocalypse.

Thank you to the angel who first suggested warming blankets in hospitals.

Thank you nurses and techs at the core of my care.

Thank you doctors who manage to practice medicine in spite of ever changing studies.

Thank you Cheri and Christian, two brilliant women who lent me their brain power when mine was otherwise engaged.

Thank you to friends who rallied to feed my family, and to Donna who made my youngest feel cozy while mom was visiting doctors.

Thank you to my early readers, Bel, June, Brad and Karina.

Thank you to my little family at Roadtripper Ranch, my parents, my sister and brother, all fifteen nieces and nephews, and my extended family- all over the country but held close in our hearts.

Thank you JDB for patiently waiting for me to finish this story all those nights, before I could read you yours.

Danielli, mille grazii per tutti. Sempre cosi.

About the Author

Kimberly Davis Basso is a playwright, director and producer who lives in the Los Angeles area with one husband, two children, two dogs, and one cat. When she is not writing, she dabbles in planning for the zombie apocalypse, in a very, very casual way. She doesn't actually have extra soup on hand, but she thinks it's a good idea. That or a moat. Her other books and plays can be found at her website, KimberlyDavisBasso.com and she can be reached via email KDBassoWrites@gmail.com, Twitter @KDBWrites and Instagram KDBWrites.

Please contact Kimberly to share your own brain dead moments, #imalittlebraindead. Subscribers to her email list receive sneak peaks and previews of her upcoming works, including the prequel to this book, *Birth and Other Surprises*.

If you enjoyed this book, please review it. If you didn't enjoy it, please recommend it to someone you don't like.

~

Back cover photo credit:
Donna Alberico
www.DonnaAlberico.com

CPSIA information can be obtained
at www.ICGtesting.com
Printed in the USA
FSHW020904150220
67090FS